"In *The Road Within* remarkable wri
experiences from every corner of the
wonder…radiant expansions of wha
—*NAPRA Review*

"The selections in *The Road Within* have two things in common:
They are all beautifully written, with sometimes lyrical prose; and
their authors all managed to escape mundane existence to taste,
however briefly, the cosmic consciousness." —*FATE*

"*The Spiritual Gifts of Travel* will leave the reader refreshed and
renewed.... These tales will inspire and enlighten readers and remind
them of the joys and importance of transformation through travel."
—*ForeWord*

"Travelers are usually searching for something within themselves
just as much as they're exploring some new spot on the map, a point
eloquently made in many of these tales of spiritual and personal
adventure in *Pilgrimage: Adventures of the Spirit*." —*Utne Reader*

"The selections in *The Ultimate Journey* transcend religious,
geographic, and cultural boundaries; dozens of contributing authors
bring astonishingly varied points of view. The book is uplifting,
enchanting, and inspiring. We plan to keep this provocative book in
stock on an ongoing basis." —*New Age Retailer*

"*The Ultimate Journey* is a glorious collection of writings about the
ultimate adventure: into the mysteries of the human spirit. The range
of essays here is as breathtaking as the quality, as near-death experience, Indian astrology, World War II, Tibetan ritual and a host of other
topics provide glimpses, through the splendid prose of such authors as
Barry Lopez, Barbara Kingsolver, and Pico Iyer, into the elusive meaning of life and death. One leaves this book with boundless admiration
for the courage and kindness of human beings, and for renewed love
for the cosmos in which we dwell. A book to keep by one's bedside—
and close to one's heart." —Philip Zaleski, author of *Gifts of the Spirit*

Other Spiritual Titles

The Road Within:
True Stories of Transformation and the Soul
Edited by Sean O'Reilly, James O'Reilly, and Tim O'Reilly

Pilgrimage:
Adventures of the Spirit
Edited by Sean O'Reilly and James O'Reilly

The Ultimate Journey:
Inspiring Stories of Living and Dying
Edited by James O'Reilly, Sean O'Reilly, and Richard Sterling

The Spiritual Gifts of Travel:
The Best of Travelers' Tales
Edited by James O'Reilly and Sean O'Reilly

The Sword of Heaven:
A Five Continent
Odyssey to Save the World
By Mikkel Aaland

A Woman's Path:
Women's Best Spiritual Travel Writing
Edited by Lucy McCauley

The Way of the Wanderer:
Discover Your True Self Through Travel
Written and Illustrated by David Yeadon

Stories to Live By

Wisdom to Help You Make the Most of Every Day

Stories to Live By

WISDOM TO HELP YOU MAKE THE MOST OF EVERY DAY

Edited by

JAMES O'REILLY

SEAN O'REILLY

LARRY HABEGGER

Solas House
Imprint of Travelers' Tales

Solas House is an imprint of Travelers' Tales. Solas House and Travelers' Tales are trademarks of Travelers' Tales, Inc., 853 Alma Street, Palo Alto, California, 94301. www.travelerstales.com

Art Direction: Stefan Gutermuth
Interior Design: Melanie Haage
Page Layout: Melanie Haage using the fonts Minion and Papyrus.

Distributed by: Publishers Group West, 1700 Fourth Street, Berkeley, California 94710

LIBRARY OF CONGRESS CATALOGING-IN-PUBLICATION DATA

Stories to live by : wisdom to help you make the most of every day / edited by James O'Reilly, Sean O'Reilly, Larry Habegger.— 1st ed.
    p.   cm.
 ISBN 1-932361-20-0 (pbk.)
 1. Interpersonal relations—Case studies. 2. Quality of life. 3. Conduct of life. 4. Social values. I. O'Reilly, James, 1953- II. O'Reilly, Sean. III. Habegger, Larry.
 HM1106.S766 2005
 158.1'28—dc22   2005016882

First Edition
Printed in the United States of America
10 9 8 7 6 5 4 3 2 1

For those inestimable Hillams—
Anne, Peg, Maureen, and Walter

Table of Contents

Introduction
by Cecile Andrews

"What if one's life were not a commodity, not something to be bartered to the highest bidder, or made to order?"

So begins one of the essays in this wonderful volume. It's a question each one of us must answer. What if we resisted the commodification of life in our times, what if we refused to sell our souls?

That's what these stories are about: resisting the forces that make life sterile, empty, lonely, and meaningless; engaging in behaviors that help us live life more deeply and ecstatically.

These stories are by and about people who resist the strongest current of the twenty-first century—the pursuit of false values and the resulting psychic numbing. You feel something truly authentic when you read these stories. Each has a narrative that captures and engages us, evoking emotions with intensity and aliveness. There's nothing here about someone getting a promotion or winning the lottery or making lots of money. They are all about life-changing experiences of human connection—of kindness and honesty and risk. It's rare today, in this age of constant and perpetual interruptions, to have this essential, satisfying human experience of being absorbed by the beauty and wisdom of others.

While these themes of human transcendence and connection are eternal, they are particularly significant now. In the last forty years, happiness in the United States has declined and depression has spiked. One prominent cause is a decline in warm, caring relationships. Psychologists have found that the biggest predictor of physical and emotional well-being is close relationships, and in the last forty years, meaningful time spent with others has diminished, and is continuing to diminish as the world rushes to embrace technology and speed at the expense of family and friends and living in the moment.

You can read a statistic like that, but the force of it is brought home in this volume. Here you experience life-giving encounters with others. Some accounts sweep you away, like Terry Tempest Williams's story of her love for her brain-damaged uncle, or Maya Angelou's story of her teenage pregnancy, or Rachel Naomi Remen's story of a young man with cancer. Others are just as inspiring—such as the one by the corporate executive who quit his secure job to live in Big Sur; or the young woman who bought a van and headed out for a year's worth of adventures; or the death row inmate who was transformed by a visit from Mother Teresa.

Even though all the stories are of personal experiences, many emerge from the most significant events of our times. There's the story of French villagers who hid Jews during World War II, the account of an angry Vietnam veteran who was transformed by Buddhist teacher Thich Nat Hahn's ideas, Victor Frankel's essay about the vision of his wife that kept him alive in a concentration camp. These are someone else's stories, but they give us comfort and insight into our own lives. Who hasn't had a tragedy that has touched them? These stories help you find meaning in your own suffering.

And this is so terribly important. We must find and apply the meaning in our experiences; our values must be rooted in our real lives, if we are to resist all the forces that manipulate our emotions— from advertising to politicians to churches and schools. The stories in this book show us how to read our own lives and discover our own wisdom. They inspire us to live more fully, anchored by more than the struggle to get ahead in a consumer culture.

I read a lot of sociology, psychology, and history. But I can't go without stories. Good stories are the one sure way to both lose yourself and find yourself. On one hand, you could say that we're flooded with stories these days—particularly from television. But most of them offer only fake friends, counterfeit emotions, and ersatz wisdom. The stories in this book are real; the emotions evoked are real. They rekindle the sense that *so much more is possible* in the way we live our lives, in every moment, in each contact with others.

Kurt Vonnegut's description of his daily life perhaps says it best—taking his time, moving slowly and chatting with people as he meanders through his day. His advice to us: "And I tell you, we are here on Earth to fart around, and don't let anybody tell you any different."

This kind of playfulness and humor may be the best way to resist the commodification of our lives and to experience our days deeply and fully.

Cecile Andrews (www.cecileandrews.com) is the author of *The Circle of Simplicity: Return to the Good Life.* She works with the Simplicity Movement, a way of life encouraging people to make conscious choices about they way they live, stripping away the inessential so the essential comes through, and finding less stress and more fun. She and her husband, Paul Andrews (author of *Gates* and *How the Web Was Won*) are founding members of an urban ecovillage in Seattle, working to encourage sustainability for people and the planet (www.phinneyecovillage.net). Cecile is a community educator and has her doctorate in education from Stanford University.

The Butterfly Man

MARK GRUBER, O.S.B.

There is a famous zoologist, a famous scientist who studies of all things, butterflies. His name is Jonathan Weiner. Jonathan Weiner is one of the foremost authorities on the butterfly in the world today, and he came to this interest when he was in college. Actually he was a biology major. But one springtime afternoon he skipped classes with a sense of restlessness and climbed out upon a hill overlooking the college. And he sat down in a field and fell asleep.

Several hours later he felt something brush against his face and he woke up, well, half woke. And in that half-awake experience he saw a blur of colors above his face—white and orange and yellow and black—and he couldn't quite define what it was. When he reached out his hand to touch it, it receded from his grasp. And when it took a little distance, he realized it was a pack of monarch butterflies which had been congregating all around him. Now Jonathan said at that moment when the butterflies receded from his grasp, he experienced a strong and painful sense of beauty and urgency. He said there was in his heart a terrible sense of yearning, and he didn't know why. But he watched the monarchs as they flew away and became so impressed with them, so mesmerized by them, that he went back to the university and decided that he was going to study animals and insects for the rest of his life.

Years later Jonathan Weiner went home and visited his parents over a vacation. And while he was there, he went up into the attic with his father to clean it with him. They came to the old crib in which he had once slept as a baby. And hanging above the crib he noticed for the first time—he had no recollection of ever seeing it before—there was one of those mobiles, those hanging toys which are placed above the cribs of children—thirty or forty colorful butterflies hanging from strings. And he said to his father, "Was this hanging over my head when I was a baby?"

"Yes," his father said, "your mother put it there. It was there for the first six months of your life. You kept reaching for it; you kept trying to grasp it; it was always a little bit too high for you. The saddest thing was that when you finally were able to reach it, your mother was afraid that you would hurt yourself on the edges of the butterflies, so she removed it. Too bad, I always thought. You never got to touch those butterflies that were hanging over your head."

Jonathan Weiner began to meditate on this experience—that perhaps when he was a student, he was actually remembering from some place deep in his soul, the sign, the picture, the color of those butterflies which were hanging over his crib eighteen or nineteen years earlier. Perhaps so.

Weiner remembers a French philosopher who once said: The project of our life is none other than this: To recover by any way possible, by music, by art, by dance—to recover by any way possible—those simple images by which our hearts were first opened.

Father Mark Gruber is a Benedictine monk at St. Vincent Archabbey in Latrobe, Pennsylvania, who is currently teaching classes in anthropology at St. Vincent College. He received a B.A. in Philosophy and an M. Div. from St. Vincent College and Seminary, and an M.A. and a Ph.D. in Anthropological Sciences from the University of New York at Stony Brook. He also gives retreats, and provides spiritual direction to both the religious and the laity.

The Reality Test

ROBERT FULGHUM

It was the summer of 1959. At a resort inn in the Sierra Nevada of Northern California, I had a job that combined being the night desk clerk in the lodge and helping with the horse-wrangling at the stables. The owner-manager was Swiss, with European notions about conditions of employment. He and I did not get along. I thought he was a fascist who wanted peasant employees who knew their place. I was twenty-two, just out of college, and pretty free with my opinions.

One week the employees had been served the same thing for lunch every single day. Two wieners, a mound of sauerkraut, and stale rolls. To compound insult with injury, the cost of the meals was deducted from our paychecks. I was outraged.

On Friday night of that awful week, I was at my desk job around 11 P.M., and the night auditor had just come on duty. I went into the kitchen and saw a note to the chef to the effect that wieners and sauerkraut were on the employee menu for two more days. That did it. For lack of any better audience, I unloaded on the night auditor, Sigmund Wollman. I declared that I had had it up to here, that I was going to get a plate of wieners and sauerkraut and wake up the owner and throw it at him. Nobody was going to make me eat wieners and sauerkraut for a whole week and make me pay for it and this was un-American and I didn't like wieners and sauerkraut enough to eat them one day for God's sake and the whole hotel stunk and I was packing my bags and heading for Montana where they never even heard of wieners and sauerkraut and wouldn't feed that stuff to pigs. Something like that.

I raved on in this way for twenty minutes. My monologue was delivered at the top of my lungs, punctuated by blows on the front desk with a fly swatter, the kicking of chairs, and much profanity.

As I pitched my fit, Sigmund Wollman sat quietly on his stool, watching me with sorrowful eyes. Put a bloodhound in a suit and tie and you have Sigmund Wollman. He had good reason to look sorrowful. Survivor of Auschwitz. Three years. German Jew. Thin, coughed a lot. He liked being alone at the night job. It gave him intellectual space, peace and quiet, and, even more, he could go into the kitchen and have a snack whenever he wanted to—all the wieners and sauerkraut he wished. To him, a feast. More than that, there was nobody around to tell him what to do. In Auschwitz he had dreamed of such a time. The only person he saw at work was me, the nightly disturber of his dream. Our shifts overlapped an hour. And here I was, a one-man war party at full cry.

"Lissen, Fulchum. Lissen me, lissen me. You know what's wrong with you? It's not wieners and kraut and it's not the boss and it's not the chef and it's not this job."

"So what's wrong with me?"

"Fulchum, you think you know everything, but you don't know the difference between an inconvenience and a problem. If you break your neck, if you have nothing to eat, if your house is on fire—then you got a problem. Everything else is inconvenience. Life *is* inconvenient. Life *is* lumpy.

"Learn to separate the inconveniences from the real problems. You will live longer. And not annoy people like me so much. Good night." In a gesture combining dismissal and blessing, he waved me off to bed.

Seldom in my life have I been hit between the eyes so hard with truth. There in that late-night darkness of a Sierra Nevada inn, Sigmund Wollman simultaneously kicked my butt and opened a window in my mind.

For many years now, in times of stress and strain, when something has me backed against the wall and I'm ready to do something really stupid with my anger, a sorrowful face appears in my mind and asks, "Fulchum. Problem or inconvenience?" I think of this as the Wollman Test of Reality. Life is lumpy. And a lump in the oatmeal, a lump in the throat, and a lump in the breast are not the same lump. One should learn the difference. Good night, Sig.

Robert Fulghum is the author of the best-selling books *All I Really Need to Know I Learned in Kindergarten* and *It Was on Fire When I Lay Down on It.*

One Man Down, One Species Up

BRAD NEWSHAM

I had just dropped a conventioneer from North Carolina at the Fillmore Auditorium, when on the sidewalk over to my left I saw a white man down on his knees, in obvious distress, clinging to a lamppost as if it were the mast of a sinking yacht. An Asian woman was hurrying toward him, a look of concern on her face, one arm outstretched. I made a U-turn, stopped my cab thirty feet from the man, got out, lowered my wheelchair ramp and walked over.

Three or four people were beside him now. A young Tibetan-looking fellow had his hand on the white man's shoulder and was murmuring some things I couldn't hear. On the pavement in the circle of light surrounding us, I noticed two plastic bags of groceries from the nearby Safeway.

The man, a big, tall, husky guy, appeared to be about fifty-five or sixty, a retired logger, I imagined, who'd recently put on some weight. After a life spent humping a chain saw up and down hills and jumping clear of crashing timber, he now looked beat up, bloated. His hair had gone to strands, his blue eyes were watery, and his red, puffy face was in full grimace. Through gritting teeth he said, "If I can just get my leg straight."

I gripped under his armpit. The Tibetan guy and the Asian woman and now two young black men and two more Asian women all grabbed other spots on the white man, and together we gave a big heave. Halfway up, the man reclaimed his own weight and the rest of us relaxed, but suddenly his legs buckled and in spite of our quick snatches at him he crumpled and slid back down the pole onto both knees again.

"Call ambulance!" said one of the Asian women.

A crowd had gathered around us, and a man thrust out a cell phone: "¿Telefono?"

"No, no," the white man said. "This is not as bad as it looks. It's happened before. If I can get my leg straight everything'll be O.K."

"If you can make it to my taxi," I said, "I'll take you wherever you're going."

He shook his head and pointed at the highrise across Fillmore Street. "I live right there. I just need to get my left knee out straight."

Wordlessly, the two black men grabbed him under his thighs and hoisted him two feet off the ground. The Asian women and I steadied his torso. The Tibetan guy unfolded the man's left leg, and a skinny, long-haired white kid who'd suddenly materialized unfolded the right, and we all lowered him down onto his buttocks. Sitting up now, with his balky legs finally stretched out in front of him on the sidewalk, he let go of the pole and sighed: "That's a lot better. "

No one rushed him.

A moment later the man said, "If I could just stand up…" Now everyone, including all onlookers, shifted into position as effortlessly as a kaleidoscope being given a simple twist. With five or six of us lined up on either side of him, lifting, the man came right up like a high-speed elevator.

"Oh, yeah," he said. "Oh, yeah."

No one let go until he locked his legs and took a few practice steps. He caught his breath, gathered himself, bent to pick up his groceries—but a dozen hands beat him to it.

The novelist Ann Tyler once suggested that if extraterrestrials were to land near a hospital emergency entrance and see all the white-clad attendants rushing out to assist the incoming injured, they would surmise that human beings were the most caring, most loving species in the entire universe.

The man shuffled off toward his highrise. The 22-Fillmore swept into the bus stop across the street and the two black guys and the Tibetan trotted after it.

The Asian women silently reclaimed their own bags and scattered. I retrieved my cab's wheelchair ramp. On the radio the dispatcher was saying there was a call waiting over in Zone 56.

Brad Newsham is a San Francisco cab driver and author of two round-the-world travel memoirs—*All the Right Places* and *Take Me With You.* On September 11, 2002, he founded Backpack Nation, an organization whose aim is to dispatch globe-roaming ambassadors to act as agents of peace in the world. For more information or to contact Brad, go to www.backpacknation.org or www.bradnewsham.com.

The Container

RACHEL NAOMI REMEN, M.D.

Often anger is a sign of engagement with life. People who are angry are touched deeply by the events of their lives and feel strongly about them. As an emotion, it has its limitations and it certainly has very bad press, but my experience with ill people suggests that there is something healthy about it. Certainly the cancer studies by Levy, Temoshak, and Greer suggest that many people who recover become angry first. Anger is just a demand for change, a passionate wish for things to be different. It can be a way to reestablish important boundaries and assert personal integrity in the face of a body- and life-altering disease. And, as it was for me, it may be the first expression of the will to live. Anger becomes a problem for people only when they become wedded to it as a way of life.

One of the angriest people I have ever worked with was a young man with osteogenic sarcoma of the right leg. He had been a high school and college athlete and until the time of his diagnosis, his life had been good. Beautiful women, fast cars, personal recognition. Two weeks after his diagnosis, they had removed his right leg above the knee. This surgery, which saved his life, also ended his life. Playing ball was a thing of the past.

These days there are many sorts of self-destructive behaviors open to an angry young man like this. He refused to return to school. He began to drink heavily, to use drugs, to alienate his former admirers and friends, and to have one automobile accident after the other. After the second of these, his former coach called and referred him to me.

He was a powerfully built and handsome young man, profoundly self-oriented and isolated. At the beginning he had the sort of rage that felt very familiar to me. Filled with a sense of injustice and self-pity, he hated all the well people. In our second meeting, hoping to encourage him to show his feelings about himself, I gave him a drawing pad and asked him to draw a picture of his body. He drew a crude sketch of a vase, just an outline. Running through the center of it he drew a deep crack. He went over and over the crack with a black crayon, gritting his teeth and ripping the paper. He had tears in his eyes. They were tears of rage. It seemed to me that the drawing was a powerful statement of his pain and the finality of his loss. It was clear that this broken vase could never hold water, could never function as a vase again. It hurt to watch. After he left, I folded the picture up and saved it. It seemed too important to throw away.

In time, his anger began to change in subtle ways. He began one session by handing me an item torn from our local newspaper. It was an article about a motorcycle accident in which a young man had lost his leg. His doctors were quoted at length. I finished reading and looked up. "Those idiots don't know the first thing about it," he said furiously. Over the next month he brought in more of these articles, some from the paper and some from magazines: a girl who had been severely burned in a house fire, a boy whose hand had been partly destroyed in the explosion of his chemistry set. His reactions were always the same, a harsh judgment of the well-meaning efforts of doctors and parents. His anger about these other young people began to occupy more and more of our session time. No one understood them, no one was there for them, no one really knew how to help them. He was still enraged, but it seemed to me that underneath this anger a concern for others was growing. Encouraged, I asked him if he wanted to do anything about it. Caught by surprise, at first he said no. But, just before he left he asked me if I thought he could meet some of these others who had suffered injuries like his.

People came to our teaching hospital from all over the world, and the chances were good that there were some with the sorts of injuries that mattered to him. I said that I thought it was quite possible and I would look into it. It turned out to be easy. Within a few weeks, he had begun to visit young people on the surgical wards whose problems were similar to his own.

He came back from these visits full of stories, delighted to find that he could reach young people. He was often able to be of help when no one else could. After a while he felt able to speak to parents and families, helping them to better understand and to know what was needed. The surgeons, delighted with the results of these visits, referred more and more people to him. Some of these doctors had seen him play ball and they began to spend a little time with him. As he got to knew them, his respect for them grew. Gradually his anger faded and he developed a sort of ministry. I just watched and listened and appreciated.

My favorite of all his stories concerned a visit to a young woman who had a tragic family history: Breast cancer had claimed the lives of her mother, her sister, and her cousin. Another sister was in chemotherapy. This last event had driven her into action. At twenty-one she took one of the only options open at that time—she had both her breasts removed surgically.

He visited her on a hot midsummer day, wearing shorts, his artificial leg in full view. Deeply depressed, she lay in bed with her eyes closed, refusing to look at him. He tried everything he knew to reach her, but without success. He said things to her that only another person with an altered body would dare to say. He made jokes. He even got angry. She did not respond. All the while a radio was softly playing rock music. Frustrated, he finally stood, and in a last effort to get her attention, he unstrapped the harness of his artificial leg and let it drop to the floor with a loud thump. Startled, she opened her eyes and saw him for the first time. Encouraged, he began to hop around the room, snapping his fingers in time to the music and laughing out loud. After a moment she burst out laughing, too. "Fella," she said, "if you can dance, maybe I can sing."

This young woman became his friend and began to visit people in the hospital with him. She was in school and she encouraged him to return to school to study psychology and dream of carrying his work further. Eventually she became his wife, a very different sort of person from the models and cheerleaders he had dated in the past. But long before this, we ended our sessions together. In our final meeting, we were reviewing the way he had come, the sticking points and the turning points. I opened his chart and found the picture of the broken vase that he had drawn two years before. Unfolding it, I asked him if he remembered the drawing he had made of his body. He took it in his hands and looked at it for some time.

"You know," he said, "it's really not finished." Surprised, I extended my basket of crayons toward him. Taking a yellow crayon, he began to draw lines radiating from the crack in the vase to the very edges of the paper. Thick yellow lines. I watched, puzzled. He was smiling. Finally he put his finger on the crack, looked at me, and said softly, "This is where the light comes through."

Suffering is intimately connected to wholeness. The power in suffering to promote integrity is not only a Christian belief, it has been a part of almost every religious tradition. Yet twenty years of working with people with cancer in the setting of unimaginable loss and pain suggests that this may not be a teaching or a religious belief at all but rather some sort of natural law. That is, we might learn it not by divine revelation but simply through a careful and patient observation of the nature of the world. Suffering shapes the life force, sometimes into anger, sometimes into blame and self-pity. Eventually it may show us the freedom of loving and serving life.

Rachel Naomi Remen, M.D., is a pioneer in training physicians in relationship-centered care and has been in the private psycho-oncology practice for the past twenty years. This story was excerpted from her book, *Kitchen Table Wisdom: Stories That Heal.*

We Shall Live Again

DAVID YEADON

Deep in the mountains of Oregon, way back in the Klamath Ranges, I'd journeyed on backroads so faint and occasionally nonexistent that I wondered if I'd ever find my way out again. I wasn't exactly lost. Or maybe I was. Maybe I wanted to be lost, to be utterly vulnerable, to be open to whatever came along, to test my faith in fate once again.

And what came along was quite remarkable.

He was an old Indian. No, not a "Native American." He laughed at such PC phraseology. "White man's guilt," he called it and chuckled behind broken teeth. His face was deep mahogany brown, his skin as wrinkled and weathered and tough as rhino hide, and his smile bright enough to illuminate a football stadium.

It was the smile that made me stop the camper and walk over to meet him. He was sitting near the side of the track on a large boulder, dressed in worn jeans, a big woolen sweater, and a purple bandanna over which his gray, wiry hair fell guru-like in matted tresses down to his shoulder blades.

I think I saw his smile before I really saw him. Maybe a trickle of sunlight caught his teeth. Who knows? But first came that great grin and then came Bill.

Bill! I was disappointed by his name, hoping for Eagle-Rising or Catch-Bear-for-Breakfast or Coyote-Calling or something a bit more Indianlike. But Bill it was and Bill it remained. He said he was some subtribe of Cherokee I'd never heard of. He pointed up through the trees to a cabin perched high atop a rock outcrop on the ridgeline of the mountain. He asked if I was thirsty. I wasn't but I said I was, so he led the way slowly up through the thick undergrowth between towering pines to his lonely aerie.

The vistas were incredible. All the way south down endless serrated ranges. The receding lines of hills blurred into warm blue mists. Two bald eagles soared on spirals, barely moving their wings—just gliding in great upward circles of flight.

He offered me water and then boiled up some concoction on an outdoor stove. He called it "tea" but it was unlike any tea I've ever drunk before or since. At first it seemed insipid—rather like the barely flavored hot water you get in the more mediocre of Chinese restaurants. But as I continued to sip from the mug slowly, watching the eagles, enjoying the amazing views and peering down into shadowy valleys and canyons, something began to work its magic. I felt increasingly thirsty and the more I drank of the tea the more its flavor expanded into a spectral array of tastes, from the tartest of lemons to the sweetest of sweets I've ever experienced. Its aroma was of lavender, rose petals, and peaches; its taste was more complex but somewhere in the mix seemed raisins, oranges, honey, and mint. The rest was indefinable. But it was wonderful and I felt wonderful and Bill just sat there sipping and grinning and grinning and sipping.

Our silence was full of fellowship. It seemed to go on for hours. No talk. Just tea-sipping and gazing. No mind-yammer either for a change. Just each moment. Perfect, whole, and complete in itself.

Eventually there was conversation of a kind. He talked of the mountains, of a tribal powwow he'd attended (no whites invited) a week or so ago, of the songs and the chantings that had stretched on through whole days and nights.

I asked him if he could sing one or two of the songs. He grinned as if he knew that's precisely what I'd ask and began by beating a stick in the dust at his feet, making a soft puckering kind of sound like distant drums, drums heard far away somewhere deep in the heart of the forest.

The sound and rhythm were hypnotic. At first it was a simple beat but as he continued it seemed to develop subtle counter-rhythms and a backbeat and the foot-shuffle hiss of flesh on soft sand (with my eyes closed it really sounded like scores of feet, all shuffle dancing together).

And slowly he began to sing. Long plaintive lines, initially minor variations on a drone, in a deep monotone, but gradually expanding into higher registers, becoming plaintive, then stern and proud, then whispery, then sadly plaintive again as if beseeching something, asking for some special favor, for grace and generosity from...what?...the power of the earth, the sky? I wasn't sure. At least, not until much later.

But it was enough just to listen without having to "understand." Bill's face was lifted up toward the sun. The golden light of early evening etched the leathery puckers of his cheeks and gave the creases deep glowing shadows. His eyes were closed. Sometimes he was grinning, exuding utter happiness. Other times, in the softer plaintive passages, his face was devoid of expression as if he were opening himself up wide to receive whatever favors were to be bestowed upon him.

The faintest of breezes blew across the ridge, nudging fallen leaves and cooling us as we sat together, me with my tea and Bill with his songs and his tapping stick. And if I listened, really listened, I could hear the echoes of other voices, voices in unison, in a kind of earthy harmony, a harmony resonant with the earth and all the mysteries and powers and wonders contained within the earth.

Later, much later, I asked Bill if he could tell me what one of the songs meant—a particularly beautiful song with a fluid melodic line and a note at the end of some of the lines that was like no other note I'd ever heard—a quarter tone, like the songs I'd heard so often in Iran. Or something else, a note not capable of placement on a page of written music. It was eerie and beautiful and seemed to have the ability to hang almost tangibly in the air long after he had moved on to other song lines.

"The words are simple," he said and grinned and I knew he didn't believe that at all. And I knew that they expressed the soul and spirit of ancient cultures, now almost destroyed and lost. And I knew—just by the sound of the music and those elusive grace notes—that they reflected a total, all-encompassing understanding of the way of all life—of a world in which man exists in harmony with all living and inanimate things and is part of the natural timeless rhythm which shapes and nurtures his environment and his whole existence. These songs were not contrived for idle amusement and entertainment, neither were they sung for the benefit of a few discerning listeners. For thousands upon thousands of years (just pause and think of that, particularly in relation to our own neophyte American culture barely a couple of centuries old) they were part of the tribal fabric, the melding force of ancient peoples, full of meaning, power, and deep spiritual resonance—direct communications with the infinite.

I was an eager student and I think Bill could sense that. I asked him to tell me the words of some of his songs. He smiled, nodded as if he knew I'd ask that, too, and began with the shortest of songs—the haiku-like "Eagle's Song" (three simple lines, repeated and repeated):

The sun's rays
Lie along my wings
And stretch beyond their tips

Then he again sang the "Corn Song":

> The corn grows up
> The waters of the dark clouds drop, drop.
> The rain descends.
> The waters from the corn leaves drop, drop.
> The rain descends.
> The waters from the plains drop, drop.
> The corn grows up.
> The waters of the dark mists drop, drop.

And then "The Rock":

> Unmoved
> From time without end,
> You rest in the midst of the coming winds,
> In the winds
> You rest, aged one.
> Small grasses grow around you
> You are covered with the droppings of the birds,
> Your top decked with downy feathers.
> Oh, aged one.

Then another short haiku:

> I am simply on the earth
> Need I be afraid?

And then the most beautiful song of all, "The Mountain Chant," the one with those strange plaintive notes:

> In beauty may I walk.
> All day long may I walk.

Through the returning seasons may I walk.
On the trail marked with pollen may I walk.
With grasshoppers about my feet may I walk.
With dew about my feet may I walk.
With beauty may I walk.

And finally he sang again the most powerful short song of all, chanted endlessly—"The Ghost Dance":

We shall live again.
We shall live again.

Evening was creeping in quickly now over the purpling ridges and I realized that I had to find my way out of the mountains on that elusive back road before dark.

I thanked Bill for his kindness and his company and then asked a question that I hadn't intended to ask. It just sort of appeared: "That last song. 'The Ghost Dance.' 'We shall live again.' Do you really believe that?"

Once again that grin. All-enveloping. All-embracing. "Yes," Bill replied simply, grinning that grin.

"But how?" I asked. "When so few Indians—so few of you—are left?"

Bill didn't respond to that one. He just grinned wider than ever—looked right into my eyes, deeper, deeper than anyone had looked before, and something inside me suddenly opened up—like a box, long locked and now unlocked. And I felt as if he'd placed not only all the songs he'd sung for me into that box but the spirit behind the songs, the ancient, timeless knowledge that gave those songs their all-encompassing life and power.

And as I walked down the path from his tiny ridge-top cabin I felt myself filled with enormous richness and energy and vitality and the words of the "Ghost Dance" seemed to surround me and permeate every particle of my being. I heard the words as clearly as if Bill were singing them beside me. And I heard something else. I heard Bill's voice inside me saying, "We shall live again.... We shall live again."

And I knew how, too.

A native of Yorkshire, England, David Yeadon has worked as an author, illustrator, journalist, and photographer for more than twenty-five years. He is the author of numerous books including, *National Geographic Guide to the World's Secret Places, Seasons in Basilicata, The Back of Beyond, Lost Worlds,* and *The Way of the Wanderer,* from which this piece was excerpted. He is also a regular travel correspondent for *National Geographic, National Geographic Traveler, The Washington Post,* and *The New York Times.* Between travels he lives with his wife, Anne, in Japan, where she is a Professor in Vision Rehabilitation, and also in a Hudson Valley lakeside house, just far enough north of Manhattan to preserve soul and sanity.

First Flight

LARRY HABEGGER

Sometimes the simplest thing can shake you loose from your moorings and show you the world again through fresh eyes. I was daydreaming at 30,000 feet above the Pacific with Pachelbel's Canon in D wafting through my headphones when we ruffled through light turbulence. I looked out the window to a world of blue sky, blue sea, and wispy white clouds, and suddenly the wonder of what we were doing struck me. We were flying.

We're among the first generations in all of human history to be able to do this, and most of us don't even notice. Flying has become as commonplace as rooting around the cupboard for breakfast cereal, and these days the thought of a flight is usually viewed as a tedious, cramped, and possibly dangerous necessity to get from here to there. It's not a marvel anymore, but there was a time when flying was so special the mere thought of it generated lively conversation. When I was growing up, flying was the provenance of the privileged, and though we all knew that some day we'd have the experience, flying was definitely out of the norm and as formative as a first kiss. Of course we expected that first experience to be full of awe and magic, and we knew it would be in a commercial aircraft—what other option would be open to us?

I had long forgotten my first flight, but looking out on the threads of fleece on my way to Maui it came back to me in a rush. It was as unexpected and unlikely as anything that happened in my adolescence. I was fourteen years old, pretty much behaving like a normal fourteen-year-old with the occasional push against boundaries, when a friend who was a bit more daring than I said he had a friend, an older guy named Bob, who had a private plane and would take us flying. All I had to do was meet them tomorrow after dinner and we'd go.

Of course I said yes. I was there at the appointed time, having given my parents a safe explanation for where I was heading, but my friend was not. Bob was waiting in his cherry-red Chevy Impala, but my friend never came.

I had to decide: Would I go off alone with this man in his mid-twenties whom I'd never met, hope he really did have a plane and would take me flying, and risk whatever else was on his agenda, or would I go home?

The allure was too great. I took the risk. I went with Bob. Even today I have no idea if I correctly assessed that he was a decent fellow who would do me no harm, or if I just got lucky. Looking back, my guess is he was a lonely guy in search of company, possibly gay, in a time and place where it was difficult and painful to be so.

We drove twenty minutes to an airfield on bluffs above the Minnesota River, the same airfield I had passed on the way to my grandparents' house every week since I was born. We parked in the darkness near a hanger; Bob checked the wings and tail, tires and fuel tank. We climbed aboard and strapped in. He put on his earphones and radioed the control tower. Then he started the engine.

The roar was deafening; there was no question of conversation. My heart started to gallop. Taxiing put me as close to the edge of my seat as the seatbelt allowed. Racing down the runway stole my breath. Takeoff was almost instant, barely noticeable, like coasting downhill on a new bike, absolutely out of this world.

The earth fell away. We swept up into the dark night sky, stars shedding their light from the heavens and mirrored like contrapuntal music in the lights twinkling below. Buildings diminished, cars became toys streaming light, roads mere snaking threads through the dark countryside. The wide floodplain of the river, a lush landmark that filled me with a vital sense of the natural world whenever I saw it, fell away as black velvet meandering through a carpet of lights.

We were only in the air a half-hour or so, a time that seemed both an instant and an eternity. I hardly remember breathing I was so completely enthralled. All the way home the thrill ran through me, but then I wondered, who could I share this with? I couldn't tell my parents—they'd kill me. My brothers? My friends?

In the end I didn't tell anyone, treasuring the secret as if it were sacred. I carried it so long I finally forgot it, until now.

When we made a big bank turn to prepare for our approach to Kahului, I looked out under the wing to the blue sky above, deep blue sea below, fleece scattered in between, and felt the sensation again of our craft blazing through the air on a perfect day. This wasn't a virtual thing, and it wasn't an ordinary thing: we were flying, and this time it felt as sacred and marvelous as that first flight with Bob, a man I never saw again but appreciate to this day.

Larry Habegger, executive editor of Travelers' Tales, has been writing about travel since 1980. He regularly teaches the craft of travel writing at workshops and writer's conferences, and he lives with his family in San Francisco.

Wildflowers

HARRIET HAMILTON

I walked past them as if they weren't there. Twenty years living in Mexico had given me plenty of opportunities to recognize the faces of poverty. Now, with our riverboat docked on the Russian Volga, my friends and I had a scant three hours to visit museums, see churches, and bargain for souvenirs. There was no time to consider the four elderly women who stood quietly to one side, clutching straggly bunches of wildflowers.

Several days before I had seen an old woman in Moscow, wrapped in a ragged black overcoat and huddled against the wall of a building. I had even snapped a quick photograph of her. For a second I wondered if she were faint from hunger or sick from the cold, but then I moved on. One expected to see poor people in the city. All cities had them.

That evening, back on the boat, we sat down to a beautiful dinner. A woman we had met earlier that afternoon joined us. "How did you like Uglich?" someone asked.

The woman's face clouded over. "Something happened today that I don't quite understand." She leaned over the table and lowered her voice. "I got hungry while we were out this morning and decided to snack on a roll I had taken with me from breakfast. I took it out of my purse and had only taken a bite when an old woman carrying a bunch of half-wilted wildflowers approached me. She pointed to the roll and then to herself. I showed her it was half eaten but she kept pointing. When I finally gave it to her, I thought she was going to cry." She paused. "They must not have bakeries here."

My friends and I looked at the beautiful plates in front of us. Filet mignon, artfully placed salad greens, and delicately sautéed fresh vegetables. At that moment we knew, all of us, that we could not continue to eat unconsciously, taking food for granted. We knew what we had to do.

The next morning our riverboat was scheduled to make a stop at another town. At breakfast the waiters exchanged polite if uncomprehending smiles as we loaded our pockets with extra hard-boiled eggs and containers of yogurt. We discreetly filled small plastic shopping bags with apples, rolls, and packets of jam and butter before we walked out of the dining room.

Soon after the boat docked, we walked down the gangplank, past a parade of souvenir stands and there they were, standing quietly off to one side. Not the same women, of course, but they could have been. Old babushkas, heads tied with faded cotton scarves that had seen too many washings and hands that had felt life too intensely, clutched bouquets of wilted wildflowers. One woman closed her eyes and pressed her palms together in silent prayer. But it was their eyes that told their stories. Hopeful eyes, pleading eyes, eyes that said, *It's O.K. if you can't see us; it's O.K. if you don't understand.* Smiles on their faces that didn't waver if you didn't return them. Smiles that said, *We've survived this long, it'll be all right.* Smiles that sought to soothe rather than be soothed.

Feeling self-conscious, we each approached one of the women, thrust the bags in their hands and quickly turned away, embarrassed at the gap between us. Embarrassed that we had so much and they had so little, embarrassed that our abundance meant so little and their lack meant so much.

As I walked away, an old grandmother came after me. She called and reached out, touching me on the shoulder. I turned around, afraid the gulf between us was too great and that she would mistake my compassion for pity. Strands of gray hair wandered out from beneath her kerchief. Small blue eyes met my gaze. She looked first at me, then at the small bag in her hands, then back at me, the tiny blue eyes now filled with tears. I reacted badly. I had never seen so much gratitude pour out of one human heart over a couple of pieces of bread. I didn't want her to see that I, too, was crying. I didn't want her to know how bad I felt for her and how helpless I felt. I stuffed the feeling down, forced a cheerful smile, nodded as if her poverty and her gratitude had not touched me, and quickly walked away.

Eventually we came to terms with the enormity of their poverty and the limitations of our efforts. By the time we reached the little town of Svir Stroy several days later, we thought we would surely return to the boat with our well-stocked bags. Sturdy houses shared by several families and tiny, well-tended gardens gave us an impression of relative wealth in this little town. Cows roamed in tree-lined streets, children chatted animatedly with each other, and vendors hastily set out souvenirs to take advantage of the riverboats' brief visits. We bought jars of homemade lingonberry jam and a whole smoked fish.

But June was chilly this far north, even in the Russian sunshine. And there they were, standing just beyond the vendors, off to one side. Four old women, dressed in layers of worn-out clothing, shawls draped over their shoulders, kerchiefs on their heads, hopeful smiles on their faces and wildflowers in their hands. We put our purchases aside and bought their flowers, gave them our bags of food, our smiles, and our warmest hugs. When two school girls examined an apple with more interest than an American kid would have looked at an FAO Schwartz card, we bought their simple drawings as well.

Not all the old women in Svir Stroy had to beg. Several women opened their homes and served tea. We were delighted to accept their invitations. We wanted to see their homes, to see how they lived, and to be, if only for a few moments, a part of their lives. One woman had no tea, as it turned out, but invited us in for simple store-bought cookies and homemade vodka. We sat around an old table in the room that served as living room, dining room, and bedroom while she pointed to the family photographs on the wall. We pulled out photos and pointed to our family members as well, and when we left we felt that we had both shared what was dearest to our hearts.

"Most of the older women lost their husbands and sons during the Stalin purges," our interpreter explained. "With a new regime, they also lost their pensions. Now they have nothing." I thought about the poor people I had seen so often in Mexico. I had consoled myself with the fact that there was always a fruit tree somewhere, that beans and tortillas were cheap. But Russia was not Mexico. How much food could you grow this far north in a place that only gave you three months to do it?

The rest of the trip our rooms overflowed with flowers. The faces of these old women were the first thing we looked for when we got off the boat, and their wildflowers were the first purchase we made. We bought every flower, no matter how wilted. Wildflowers of every sort filled the window, crowded the table, sat on the floor and overflowed on the shelves. If they asked one dollar, we paid three, sometimes five. We no longer waited for an invitation. We smiled first and hugged harder, sincerely wishing we could take all of them home with us.

There were several passengers on the boat who had made the same trip before. At the beginning of the cruise I had thought they were silly for taking the same trip over again when there were so many other places to see. Now I dream of going back and filling the entire boat with flowers.

Harriet Hamilton is a Spanish teacher and freelance writer who lives in Arkansas.

Just Desert

ANDREW BILL

In the course of my early travels—when a lack of money and a lot of time necessitated hitchhiking through the night, sleeping in city parks or on lonely beaches—I have gathered a store of tales enough to fill a thousand cocktail parties. I have been cornered in the solid 2 A.M. shadows of the Greyhound Bus Station in Boston by a knife-wielding Irishman who, fired by the strong spirits of his homeland, was convinced "the only good Englishman is a dead Englishman." I have been shot at in the bright-red poppy fields of the Golden Triangle where Burma, Laos, and Thailand converge to form the opium capital of the world; framed and arrested in a small tropical "prawn" town in the north of Australia where just being a foreigner was tantamount to a confession of guilt. I have been given a death sentence by a doctor high in the Himalayas, and attacked by a wave of rats on a black night in Mexico.

Yet among all these experiences there is one moment in the Sinai that stays lodged in the forefront of my memory like a bone in the throat. Remarkable not for its drama but for what it taught me about myself, it remains as fresh as the day it happened more than twenty years ago.

"Masari?"

I shrug my shoulders to tell him I don't understand. Not that word. Not any word. I can't even look it up in my dictionary. It probably isn't Egyptian at all, but one of the many Bedouin dialects.

"*Masari?*" he says again, spitting out the word like an olive pit.

I look back at him, reading his face for clues. A dusty red-and-white checked headdress obscures all but the small oval from forehead to chin. Dirt has been ironed into a thousand lines by the desert and the sun. His eyes, even in the shadow of the room, are burnt into thin rheumy slits. Untamed jet-black eyebrows hint at the color of his hair. The lips are set in what can only be impatience, rapidly dissolving into anger. I can't tell what age he is, still less what he is saying.

"*Masari?*" he almost shouts it this time, "*Masari? Felous? Felous?*" It's obviously a question. Fumbling in the folds of his tunic, he extracts a disheveled Egyptian pound and waves it in my face.

Here it is. The moment I have been expecting for the last hour. Dreading. One thing I have learned from my few years on the road is that nothing is for nothing. It's exactly proportionate: the more foreign the country, the more I am regarded as a one-man walking business opportunity. The postcard that costs 5¢ to a local, costs $1 to me. The "set price" for the taxi ride from the airport magically inflates out of control as soon as I hit an open stretch of road. I'm perpetually on guard, seeing the rip-offs as obstacles to be avoided by the savvy traveler. The few times I get badly caught, I rationalize the loss. What does a dollar mean to me, after all, compared with its power in local currency? My simple camera is worth a year's worth of meals to a starving family. I have spent more on having a tooth capped than many Third World-ers will ever amass over a lifetime of grueling labor. And yet I feel a mounting indignation swelling inside, from a sense of my own gullibility, from allowing myself to be fooled like a common tourist.

But today I have committed the cardinal blunder. My caution overpowered by two days of aching hunger, I have accepted food and hospitality from a total stranger. Worse, he is a nomad, a desert dweller, dealing from a completely different deck of customs and values. For him "taking" is the same as "earning." And I followed him home, ate everything that was offered, and never agreed on a price in advance. Stupid! Stupid! Stupid! Now he is going to levy an enormous price—somewhere between my money and my life—on a few pieces of dehydrated bread, rubbery meat, and a tomato sucked dry by the sun. And the spirit in the sheep-bladder bottle would strip paint. Considering my choices, I look around the room.

We are sitting in what had been, just four months before, the living room of a modern, luxury condo. The place has been stripped to the bare walls leaving only a few hints of its former style. Chrome light fixtures in the shape of medieval torchieres hang upside down from wires as though someone had ripped them down in a hurry and given up half-way through. There is no electricity anyway. The broken-in door swings awkwardly on its hinges. The window panes are all broken and, caught by the late afternoon breeze off the sea, floral curtains wave out like flags. Dust covers everything in a softening film. In the middle of the green wall-to-wall shag carpet burns an open campfire made of broken drawers and paneling. Around its edge, the nylon weave is curling, sending up a black-smoke stench.

Around its edge lounge five other Bedouin men, all dressed in the same robes as my host, with traditional *okal* headdresses and the *khangars* at their belts. Clearly these half-swords are not just for show. Throughout the meal these men have looked over at me with dirty, gold-toothed smiles, obviously enjoying the game of ripping off the white-skinned foreigner. It occurs to me this is a familiar situation and I am probably not the first Westerner to be sharing this room and their food. If I run for the door, surely one of them will be there to block my exit. If not, I have no doubt, they will catch up with me in the streets below. The smiles will then be gone and who knows what will follow.

Seeing no alternative, I loosen the tails of my shirt, uncover and unzip my money belt. All my valuables are now on show. My watch, passport, the few traveler's checks I have, and the thick soiled wad of local currency. Glancing quickly at my host, I see his eyes widen. With my heart in my mouth I try to offset the inevitable. I say the one Egyptian word I know, "*Bekam?*" How much?

The Sinai Peninsula is the huge triangle of desert dividing the two outstretched arms of the Red Sea. Above it teeters Israel; to the left, the great sprawl of Egypt. Its harsh, unforgiving lunar landscape is burnt as hard as a pot in a kiln. From a rugged mountainous interior, a boulder and scrub strewn terrain spills down to an unremarkable coast. One hue—beige. Until you dip one inch below the surface of the sea. As if all the color had drained into the water, there lies a marine world of unimaginable beauty.

In 1982 the Sinai was on the front page of every newspaper. After two years of "preparation," Israel had honored the terms of Begin and Sadat's Camp David accord and handed back the region to Egypt. Along with the desert, Egypt inherited all the buildings and infrastructure that had sprung up over the previous decade when the coasts along the Gulfs of Aqaba and Suez had blossomed as the Riviera of the Middle East.

Naturally there was chaos. When the Israelis left they took everything with them. Everything that could be moved, unscrewed, dismantled or otherwise heaved on to flat-bed trucks and driven north. The pans and cookers from the hotel kitchens, the sinks and doorknobs from the luxury apartments, the tiles from the walls, the contents of the luxury beach-front boutiques. And, of course they took all the food.

If I knew this at the time, I paid little attention. As a university student, my needs were simple and my tolerance for discomfort high. Besides, my interest was far more Old Testament than media front page. For me the Sinai was the romantic bridge between Africa and Asia. It was birthplace of the alphabet, the stage-set of *Exodus*, where the seas had miraculously parted for the escaping Israelites, where God had spoken from the flames of a burning bush, where Moses had found and dropped the Ten Commandments, that summary of divine law. On another, more immediate level, the Sinai was also the site of the best scuba diving in the world. Compared with this, what could possibly be so bad?

Well, there *was* the temperature. In retrospect, August was probably not the best time to be carrying a fifty-pound backpack through a desert described even by the guidebooks as "intensely hot." And there *was* the lack of any predictable transport. As I left the air-conditioned bars of Eilat, Israel, at my back and made my way on foot along the dusty road to the Egyptian border, the heat bore down on my head like a broiler, flooding the world with white heat, melting the horizon in a watery wash of quivering snakes.

At the border there were no crowds of flag-waving well-wishers, no congratulations, nothing of significance to mark my historic crossing but a few strands of barbed wire half-heartedly stretched across the road and curling off into the scrubby desert on either side. At the end of the hundred yards of no-man's land I came to the Egyptian line. To the left a soldier in a ragged uniform was sleeping off his lunch in the shade of the only tree. To the right, the border post—a banged-up shed like a Porta-Cabin.

Inside, another soldier barked a single word, "*felous*," then remembering a few words of English, he repeated, "money, money." An official-looking sheet was thrust in my hands explaining in a collection of languages that everyone who passed across the border had to change an amount of dollars proportionate to the length of stay. No exceptions. Four days? Two hundred dollars— an incredible amount which to me translated into at least twenty days of travel under normal circumstances. I handed over all the currency I had—around forty dollars—with a shrug. After a few minutes of furious tapping on a decrepit adding machine, the soldier handed back to me an inch-thick wad of notes, so soiled I could hardly make out their denominations. Doubtless, there had been a small commission for the officer's time.

I soon found out that in the Sinai it didn't matter how much money you had because there was nowhere to spend it. When the bus finally arrived a few hours later, the fare to Nuwaybi cost the smallest note in my wad. For the next few hours I sat, crammed in with a sweating mass of humanity and sundry livestock, as the bus creaked and groaned through a flat, unchanging landscape. The image of a cold beer and a good meal swam through my half-waking mind like a mantra.

But when I finally arrived in Nuwaybi, the once glamorous resort on the Gulf of Aqaba, I found that it was shut. Closed. Not open. The neat grid of streets was lined with boarded-up stores, weeds were growing rampant through the sidewalk. Eventually I managed to pick up some *falafel* (deep-fried chick pea balls) and some bread, as dehydrated as the desert itself. That night I slept on the beach, underneath the boardwalk, burrowing deep inside my oppressively hot down sleeping bag to escape the clouds of mosquitoes.

As the days followed a similar course, I began to associate more and more with the plight of the Israelites. It may not have been forty years of privation and hunger but, as I made my way south, it certainly felt like it. The towns of Dhahab and Nabq were empty shells, all the more melancholy for what they had been so recently. At least the Israelites had manna from heaven, whereas I was reduced to eating whatever I could find. A jar of jam for lunch, crackers for dinner, and one day—oh the luxury—some canned sardines. There wasn't even any diving to be had. The few dive shops that deserved the name were cobwebbed and dark, waiting for their equipment to arrive.

But it didn't matter because I had set my sights on the southernmost town of Sharm ash-Shaykh. Things would be different there, I was told. According to the guidebook, it was an oasis of civilization, studded with bars and restaurants. Furthermore it was the jumping-off point for the greatest dive site in the world. Under the surface at Ra's Muhammad, the very peak of the Sinai, the fish—hammerheads, black-tips, rays as big as bed quilts—were so plentiful, they blocked out the sun as the schools swam overhead.

Like any other mirage, the oasis of Sharm faded before my eyes, its promise evaporating into the dry sand as soon as I climbed from the bus one late afternoon. Like the towns that had gone before, an eerie vacancy haunted its main streets and beachfront, as if it was a film set waiting for the extras to arrive. Gone were the tanned couples promenading, the tables spilling out of cafés onto the street, the bikinied beauties, the cool palm-decked lobbies of the big hotels. Gone were the expensive boats, the bars heaving with the après-sun crowd. The only movement came from a few enduring old Mercedes kicking up clouds of dust and the occasional Bedouin leading camels on a tether. In the hollowed-out cavern of a store, I found a bearded German who told me, in broken English, he had come to start a scuba business but was now going back to Berlin to wait until the situation here improved. "Here there is no customers," he explained dejectedly. "If they come, they can stay nowhere, and eat nothing."

No food. I was so hungry by this stage, I was even ready to break my vow and choke down another *falafel* ball. So I started combing the back streets looking for a restaurant. The locals had to eat somewhere, didn't they? I approached a few people, but they only shook their heads or pointed off in a vague direction. It was then that I saw my Bedouin and asked him in polyglot—raising my hand to my mouth and shrugging my shoulders—if he knew of any food.

To my surprise he beckoned to me to follow. Staying thirty yards ahead of me with his long strides and flowing robes, he set off through a white maze of alleys. After each corner I became more disoriented, more and more concerned I was being led into some sort of trap. What was stopping this desert savage pulling me into a doorway and sliding his knife across my white throat? In my backpack there were surely items of clothing that would be of use or amusement. At each turn my guide turned and beckoned me on again as if anxious I would lose interest and turn around.

After fifteen minutes I was so lost, I had to keep going. Then suddenly he stopped and, without a smile, imitated my gesture of eating and pointed up some exterior stairs to an upstairs apartment in a block of luxury condos. I hesitated. He repeated the gesture and urged me on. On the second landing he pushed open a door that hung loose on its hinges; clearly it had been jimmied open. Walking into the room I smelled first the stench of singeing carpet, then, as my eyes grew accustomed to the smoke and darkness, I saw the group crouched around the fire. They looked up at us. Our friend explained and smiles broke out. Obviously they liked his plan.

For the next hour I sat aside from the main group, leaning against one of the walls. There was no attempt at conversation. Nobody spoke. In silence—as slowly and deliberately as if they always cooked their food on a fire in the middle of a carpet—the Bedouin pieced hunks of fresh meat on the end of their knives, roasted them over the embers, then slid them off onto clean slabs of paneling that one of them had ripped off the wall. After adding fresh salad and bread, my host passed a mounded plate over to me. I was too hungry to wonder where the fresh food came from, what the meat was, or what my new friends were expecting in return. Only when the meal was over and the food had cleared my head, did I realize the bad situation I was in.

"*Bekam?*" I say again, fully expecting my host to dispense with formalities, reach in and empty my money belt.

After a long minute he repeats the word at the others as if it's the biggest joke he has heard in ages. He says it again, pointing at me. The Bedouin around the fire sit up to enjoy the scene. Gold teeth glint in wide grins.

Nervously I take out one of the bigger bills and hold it out. But it's not enough. My host shakes his head. I take out more bills. Still he shakes his head. It happens a third time. Just when I'm about to hand over the entire wad, he leaps up and goes over to the air-conditioning unit below one of the windows. He struggles with it, twisting it from side to side, until it comes clear of the wall. Rummaging in the exposed insulation, he pulls out a simple black metal box and brings it over to me, placing it as gently as an egg in my hands. He signals me to open it, which I do, fearfully, bracing for a trick. It's full of money. I pick some up and look up inquiringly at the man's face. Seeing my confusion, he leans over and closes my fist around the pound notes I have drawn from the box. I look around at the others. They are smiling encouragement.

Suddenly I understand what's going on. The realization hits me like a slap. The blood rushes to my face as the great temple of my Westernized preconceptions and prejudices collapses in a heap around me. To them I am not a condescending rich kid on vacation or a gullible traveler ripe for exploitation. They simply see another nomad who is in need. They see a beggar. They are not trying to take my money. They are trying to give me theirs.

Andrew Bill is a writer living in New York.

Crime and Punishment

ELAINE MARKOWITZ

"Adolescence is difficult," was the mantra chanted by family and friends whenever our teenage daughter's behavior ran counter to all we knew of logic, proper conduct, and, at times, even sanity.

"Don't you remember your own teenage years?"

"Yes, yes, I do," I replied to those who aimed to cheer.

But I knew our daughter was not just another teenage girl going through the anxiety and emotional vacillations of a young woman in bloom. She harbored a genuine sadness that ran deeper than I could reach. I wondered if any parent truly understood the whys of a troubled teenager. I had added up and recombined all my own reasons, only to slowly discard each one.

What I didn't realize was how little it took, under the right circumstances, to diminish that sadness, allowing in the initial ray of light that would eventually dispel clouds of gloom. I had never even heard of Iris Singer before she turned our child's life around by a simple act of kindness.

I watched Michele drive off to school that morning, chugging down the street in the old maroon Buick, a hand-me-down from her grandfather. I arrived home first in the afternoon, and listened to the Buick grind to a halt in the driveway shortly thereafter.

A buoyancy in her step convinced me something positive had happened that day. And when I caught the glint of a smile in her eyes as she entered the house, I was hopeful of a change of heart— if only for a day, or even a moment.

Tucked under one arm was a thick library book; a frayed yellow placemark peeked out near the end of the book.

"What are you reading, honey?" I asked.

"*Crime and Punishment*," she answered quickly and leaped up the stairs toward her bedroom, her backpack swaying lightly as she moved.

At dinner that evening we learned about Iris Singer, a ninth-grade English teacher whom Michele, now a junior, had never had.

"She saw me reading my book in the library," Michele said, "and asked if I had to read it for English class."

"Do you?" I asked. She had never mentioned this book before, probably unaware that I, too, had read it.

"No," she said. "I'm just reading it myself." She glanced up at her father and me briefly, her fork toying with the few remaining green beans on her plate.

"No one in my class has read it, not even the teacher. Not even Mrs. Singer."

"I'm confused, honey," I said. "Did you say Mrs. Singer would read the book?"

As she responded, I sat quietly, awed by the graciousness of a teacher who agreed to read this lengthy novel, just so a student she'd never met before would have someone with whom to discuss it. Mrs. Singer had always wanted to read it anyway, Michele told us, and now a strong incentive had come her way.

"Are you sure she has time?" I asked, hoping the teacher would not disappoint our daughter. Michele's world consisted of books and music, not dates, proms, football games, or school clubs. Her adolescent years were being lived in her head. Mrs. Singer was entering sacred space.

Two weeks later our daughter asked if she could spend the following Friday night with Mrs. Singer and her husband in their condominium on the beach. Since the teacher lived some distance from both our home and the school, she had invited Michele for dinner and to sleep over. They would discuss the novel that evening, and we could pick her up on Saturday morning.

My husband and I readily agreed, grateful to see our daughter happy about the adventure and eager to share her thoughts on the brilliant but radical student, Raskolnikov, and the simple and saintly Sonia.

The following Saturday we met Mrs. Singer as she and Michele briskly approached our car, laughing and chatting as they walked.

In the days that followed I learned only that the teacher had loved the book and shown empathy for the misguided protagonist. I don't know when, or even if, Michele saw Mrs. Singer again. Sometime in the weeks that followed she told us she had given an oral book report on *Crime and Punishment*, and that a few students had expressed interest in reading it.

"After all," she said, "kids can really get into a weird student like Raskolnikov." She smiled.

The next semester Michele ran for a student council seat. She didn't win, but she seemed comfortable with the loss.

Mrs. Singer didn't work miracles. Michele still had her days of gloom, but they were far fewer. She still spent considerable time alone in her room reading or writing, but not all the time. Sometimes I heard her on the phone with her new friend, Edie.

A kind teacher had cracked open the door to a human heart and coaxed in a little warmth. With that warmth came the light of promise for our daughter and a gift for me as well—the real-ization that even a small kindness can engender the confidence a young person needs in order to cope with the many challenges strewn on the road from adolescence to adulthood.

Elaine Markowitz writes weekly features for the *Tampa Tribune*, appearing each Saturday in the Brandon section. She previously was associate editor of *Senior Connection*, a magazine for seniors that covers five Florida counties, and has been a freelance contributor to *The Christian Science Monitor*, the *St. Petersburg Times, Interfaith Family, ARMY* magazine, and a variety of other publications.

Bola's Gift

ALISON WRIGHT

Bola was the most hideously deformed man I had ever seen. Yet, even here in Calcutta, someone had loved him enough to keep him alive for twenty-three years. I was living in Nepal working as a photographer for UNICEF, Save the Children, and various other aid organizations. Over the years I had become overwhelmed by the devastation I was seeing through the lens of my camera and wanted to relate with people on a more intimate level once again. This is how I found myself working at Mother Teresa's orphanage in India.

The children at the orphanage were doe-eyed beauties in desperate need of love and attention, much like many of the other children I had been photographing throughout Asia. Frustrated nurses brusquely pinched the children's noses while trying to shove food into their mouths. One baby I held was so small I was able to cup him in the palm of my hand. His brown wrinkled skin sagged around his tiny malnourished ankles. Another baby giggled uncontrollably as I threw him into the air. "Hold that beautiful smile, you," I thought. Covered in scabs and warts, this little cherub hadn't yet realized his fate as an orphan in Calcutta.

On Easter Sunday, Mother Teresa came to visit the orphanage and attend Mass. It was hard to believe that this small shrunken woman from Albania, a face full of wrinkles, had become such a prominent symbol of all that is good in the world. Gliding into the room, she gave me a blessing and a small silver medallion of Mother Mary to wear around my neck. With a knowing smile she encouraged me to see her home of the destitute and dying. Just to visit.

The next day I hired a rickshaw to take me across town. Dripping with sweat, the rickshaw driver dropped me in front of an unpretentious building next to a bathing ghat. Working my way through the throng of people I stopped at the Kali Temple. Tended by a widowed priestess, women were tying stones and praying to a fruitless cactus tree covered with china roses in the hopes of becoming fertile. "This is a fertility tree," a woman explained to me. "We come to pray here when we have trouble giving birth." I wondered if their suffering must be part of the sacrifice. Ironically, this was right next to Kali Ghat, Mother Teresa's Home for the Destitute and Dying, where people can come and die with dignity.

And dying they were. The street was lined with the sick and elderly waiting to get inside. I nearly gagged from the pungent smell of antiseptic as I entered the building. I was immediately greeted with the sight of a nun carving the dead flesh away from a leper's foot. Dressed in flowing white robes, with blue trim, one of the nuns guided me to the women's area in the back of the building. The scene seemed as if from a concentration camp. Half-naked women with shaved heads ran from the staff and volunteers who tried to bathe them, while other patients rocked back and forth on the beds, mumbling incoherently. One woman with an open robe, exposed the fat, flesh, and bone gaping from a wound on her backside. I felt ashamed by my recoil.

We continued through the room and into the men's area. Again, the smell of antiseptic was overpowering. Men stared at me intently from their rows of green cots with the unmistakable sounds of hacking tuberculosis and vomiting. Still, I felt relieved to be away from the screeching women. There was one more bed in the corner to pass before I was finally free to head back out the door and into the chaos and sunshine. A gray-haired old man, who introduced himself as Andy Devane from Ireland, was trying to feed a much younger Indian man lying on the cot. Andy introduced him as Bola, "strong one." "He's gotten this far," Andy explained. Bola heard his name and craned his closely shaved head on the pillow to look at me. His eyes were soulful, yet imprisoned in a repulsive body, which was now flat as a Frisbee, from years of lying on a bed. His thin matchstick bones were abnormally twisted and misshapen.

"He seems taken with you," said Andy. "Why don't you try to feed him?"

This was more than I had bargained for. I was, after all, only touring the place. I wanted to return to cuddling children, not to confront illness and death to such an uncomfortable degree. Then I remembered that this was actually what my pilgrimage was about. Human connection without a camera. Globs of the pasty cereal were already dribbling from the sides of his mouth as I scooped up a spoonful of the gray gruel and tried to work it through his partially opened lips. Surprisingly, he managed to keep it down. Then another and another. Andy was amazed.

"We've been trying to feed him for days, and this is the first time he's actually been eating," said Andy incredulously. "He thinks you're an angel." Sure enough, Bola hadn't stopped staring at me since I began feeding him. "Will you please come back tomorrow? No one else has been able to get any food into him. We've been afraid that he won't make it."

And so I returned every day for the next six weeks.

Every morning I made my way through the markets in search of the ripest oranges to squeeze to make juice for Bola. I found bananas, which I mashed to a pulp. I bought Cadbury's chocolate bars, the Indian kind, made of wax, so they wouldn't melt in the heat. I crushed them down to a fine powder and fed them to Bola when the nurses weren't looking. The treats I brought became our secret. He was unable to speak, but the love pouring from his eyes spoke volumes. I wondered about the people in his life who had loved him enough to take care of him this long in such a drastically poor country, and then left him here to die. No one knew anything about his past. He was left at the doorstep like so many others.

One day I came in and Andy asked me to help him bathe a little boy who was in the bed next to Bola. We had nicknamed him Toro, "small one." I had tried to feed him, but it was no use. His skin was peeling away from malnutrition and he had a hacking bloody cough from tuberculosis. He was so ill that layers of his skin came away as Andy and I pulled off the bandages. My heart broke, as I held his bony body in my arms, trying to absorb his pain into my own. With barely the strength to wince, he put his head on my lap and whimpered. "Poor thing, he just wants a mum to hold him," said Andy. I stayed late with him, praying for him to die. But his will was so strong. Suddenly, I heard the rattle of death gurgling in his small chest. His eyes gave me a last look before they rolled back into his head and I felt his body go limp. That tiny bit of life in my arms was now free as a bird. "What an honor," said Andy. "He chose you to help him die." I should have been exuberant, but I felt overwhelmed with sadness.

I frantically looked around for a nurse, but they were all too busy to deal with this common occurrence. I thought about Andy's words. This was my responsibility. I wrapped Toro's small body in the still warm sheet, using a pin from my camera bag to close it up. Andy helped me carry him the short distance down the road to the Ganges River. We said a small prayer and dropped the body into the water.

Death is such a part of life in India. I tried to imagine dropping a body into the river in New York City, with hundreds of people watching. We walked back to the Kali Ghat home and made our way to the roof. I looked down at the senseless confusion of people below us. There was a continuous line of people waiting to get into the home. Vacancy by death only. It seemed neverending. The crush of people didn't seem jostling and exciting to me anymore. It seemed pathetic. "I just don't get it," I whispered and began to weep.

Andy put his arm around me. "You know, my wife died ten years ago. She was the sweetest woman in the world and loved me immensely, but I took her for granted. I was working as a very successful architect in Dublin. I was a philanderer and it hurt my wife greatly. One day she came home and told me that she had been diagnosed with cancer. Ironically, I had to have a triple bypass at the time, and we spent four months in the hospital together. We grew so close during that time, and it wasn't until then that I really appreciated her. She died the day I left the hospital." Andy had learned his life lessons harshly.

"After her death I gave up my job, and came here to work at Mother Teresa's full time, hoping to redeem myself. I've been here for five years. I still don't have any answers. In my room I have statues of Buddha, Ganesh, and Christ. Who knows what happens to us when we die, but I want to be sure to have my bases covered," he said with a chuckle. "All I know is, one person can't save the world. But if you touch just one person then that's something worth living for."

I returned to Calcutta a year later. Bola's bed was empty. No one there even remembered him. But I did.

Since receiving her first camera and journal at ten years old, Alison Wright has traveled from the Arctic to the Amazon documenting the traditions and changes of endangered cultures in remote areas of the world. In 1993 she received the Dorothea Lange Award in documentary photography for her photographs of child labor in Asia. Documenting Tibetan life in exile has been her project of passion for over a decade. Her published work includes *Faces of Hope: Children of a Changing World, The Spirit of Tibet: Portrait of a Culture in Exile,* and *A Simple Monk: Writings on the Dalai Lama.* View her work at www.AlisonWright.com.

A Stranger in Italy

KELLY WATTON

When I was young, my family stopped on the side of a Florida highway to help a man whose rental car had broken down on an August afternoon. The man was German, and the only word my father understood was petrol. Dad nodded and the man squeezed into the backseat of our wood-paneled station wagon alongside me and my two sisters. After taking him to a gas station, we returned and watched as he filled the tank and started the car.

Whether that incident created good karma, I can't say.

But each time I have needed help away from home, assistance has always come from a passing stranger. One such incident happened last May as my husband and I traveled through Italy. In La Spezia we boarded a train that we thought was headed to Rome. However, once we were aboard, the train pulled off in the opposite direction of where we should have been going. The compartment where our reserved seats should have been was full. It looked as if we were on the wrong train.

While my husband stood with our luggage, in a section clearly marked "no standing and no luggage storage," I walked up and down each car. *Parla inglese?* I asked of anyone who looked my way. I weaved from one car to another, working to keep my balance as the train jostled on the tracks, but I found no conductor and no hint of where the train was headed.

Frustrated, we returned to the compartment and this time found two empty seats. Although they weren't ours, we decided to sit until someone claimed them. In the meantime, my husband left to find a place to store our bags.

When he returned, he said an English-speaking man in the next compartment confirmed the train would stop in Rome. He also explained that he had left all of our luggage with him. "Don't worry," he said. "He's going to Rome and offered to watch it for us." He said the man's name was Martin, and he was in town on business, from somewhere in Africa.

A few minutes later, Martin stopped by our compartment. He was a jovial man, casually dressed in khakis and a button-down shirt. He was on his way to the dining car, and asked if he could get something for us. "Thank you, but we're headed that way shortly," my husband responded.

Before we could make our way to the car, Martin returned, handing us a bottle of red wine. "Drink it," he said. "It's good for your heart." He laughed and pounded his chest with his fist.

As the train made its way to Rome, we saw Martin a few more times. Always he asked if we were O.K. He had become our unofficial ambassador to Italy. When the train finally stopped, passengers flooded the corridors, yet Martin worked his way through the crowd to return our bags.

In the station, he introduced us to his wife, who wore a long purple dress with her hair tied in an elaborate scarf. We asked if we could take them to dinner or buy them drinks, but Martin explained they had a ride on the way. Instead, he offered to take us to our hotel.

As we stood outside the station talking, a group of official-looking men approached, each wore a small round hat and a long tunic, which hung low over their pants. Their ride, Martin explained.

He again offered to take us to our hotel, but this time the looks on the faces of his co-workers told us that wasn't a good idea. Before leaving Martin handed us his card. Our unofficial ambassador to Italy was the special assistant to the president of Nigeria.

From talking with him, we realized Martin's job requires a lot of travel. And I couldn't help but wonder if somewhere along the way, some passing stranger had watched his bags for him or picked him up when his car ran out of gas.

Kelly Watton writes travel stories for newspapers in the U.S. Thanks to her parents' constant kindness toward travelers stranded on the side of the road, she has enjoyed good karma and help from strangers in countries from South Africa to Costa Rica. She lives in Atlanta.

My Military Career

DANIEL PINKWATER

I looked up to and emulated my older brother, Marlowe. I wanted to be just like him. When I was a first-grader, Marlowe was a captain in the high school ROTC and got to wear a shiny sword on parade. It goes without saying that I wanted one, too. Later, in the Illinois National Guard, Marlowe chose not to accept a commission. Instead he rose to the rank of master sergeant. I think his decision was based in part on the fact that he looked right as a sergeant, chunky and broad-beamed. He was happy in the company office, chewing a cigar and making sure his men got ice cream in the field on maneuvers.

By the time I hit high school, cadet officers were no longer being issued swords, which was a disappointment to me. Like my noncom brother, I did no extra-credit work and remained among the ranks. Of course, having been drilled by Marlowe from the age of six, I was versed in the manual of arms, parade ground commands and military courtesy, science, and tactics. I knew by heart the names of the parts of the M1 rifle, its weight, muzzle velocity, and aspects of its trajectory. I also knew how to strip it as well as I knew how to button my coat.

As a result of being overprepared, I found the ROTC course

a trifle tedious. Also, I regret to say that the intellectual level of my fellow cadets was not impressive. It was peacetime, and unlike the period during which Marlowe had been a cadet in that very school, patriotic fervor was at a low ebb. Most of the students who signed up for ROTC in my day hoped to qualify for entrance to the Army with an eye toward a secure career—and it was painfully obvious to me that some of them were not going to make it.

Sergeant France and Sergeant Gunderson, the ROTC teachers, were fine men, and they worked hard to make something of the little cadet corps. Periodically, we'd have an exam. Numbered answers to the numbered questions would be written on a blackboard and remain there during the test. Still, more than half of the kids would fail to get a passing grade.

I remember those winter mornings in the overheated basement of the high school. The swirling fragrances of hot grease from the lunchroom and chlorine from the swimming pool, also located in the basement, would mix with the peculiar smell of soap and paint in the ROTC room. We would march up and down on the linoleum floor, or Sergeant Gunderson might drone on about sanitation in the field, while I struggled to keep my eyes open. It was a good introduction to military life, which is to say it was boredom beyond endurance.

One of the things I learned in ROTC at Lake View High School in Chicago was that the uniform I had been issued was of the maximum size, circumferentially, kept in stock by the U.S. Army. It consisted of even more wool serge than my brother's uniform at the peak of his military career. A few years later, when I made my way to an induction center, as directed by a draft notice, I had grown at least two sizes fatter and I suspected that my appearance would be entirely pro forma. Unless the Army had instituted a human-tank or land-blimp battalion, it was questionable whether they'd have any use for me.

I had graduated from college by then and moved to New York, so it was to Whitehall Street in Lower Manhattan that I had to report. Dawn was about breaking over New York Harbor when I got off the bus. The narrow streets were deserted, and I found the architecture of the oldest part of the city so fascinating that I decided to take a walk. There was no point in being precisely on time—they were sure to be milling around and getting organized for the first half-hour or so. The walk was exhilarating. The morning sun glinted on the tall buildings, and a salt breeze came off the water. By the time I reported for induction I was in a good mood.

Instantly, I was struck by familiar things: the overheated rooms, the GI colors, the linoleum, the sleepy-eyed noncoms, that smell. I was transported back to my old Chicago ROTC room. I experienced a feeling of happy nostalgia. I can handle this, I thought. If the Army could accommodate me with a big enough suit, I could accommodate the Army.

I entered a room in which inductees were sitting on benches and facing a podium at which a sergeant was addressing them about something or other. The first bench was entirely empty. I took a place, front and center.

"Please excuse me for being late," I said to the sergeant, smiling. "I took a little walk."

"What?" The sergeant glowered darkly at me.

"It's such a nice morning. I hope I didn't miss anything."

"What's your name? Sit over there and wait for the psychiatrist."

The Army psychiatrist was very nice. He explained to me that not everyone can be a soldier, and that I oughtn't to feel bad. I told him I was not disappointed and that, in a way, I felt as though I'd already had the experience. Then, excused, I went outside into the bright morning sunlight.

Daniel Pinkwater has written more than one hundred distin-
guished books, mostly for children and young people. He has
contributed articles to *Smithsonian Magazine, The New York
Times,* and the *Washington Post.* Since 1987 he has been a popular
commentator on National Public Radio. He lives with this wife,
artist Jill Pinkwater, in New York's Hudson River Valley.

Hot Like the Candle's Tip

CLAUDE THOMAS

I was trained to be a soldier from the day I was born, by the way I was brought up and the things I was encouraged to do—hunt, kill, dominate, rule, and control my environment. I was taught not to be mindful, not to be thoughtful.

My father was a schoolteacher. My mother never graduated from school. The environment in my house was not different from most of the houses around me. It was filled with anger and violence, which I did not understand because I did not have the skills to understand.

I went into the military, and then to Vietnam at the age of seventeen. I did not know what else to do, and my father suggested it would make a man out of me. I was a high school athlete, so I was already used to discipline and exerting physical strength. A local journalist said that if he had to charge a hill with anyone, he would want it to be me.

On my second day in the military, I realized it was not a good choice. But I did not know I could get out. So I did the next best thing: I learned to be the best soldier I could. I trained to be a ranger, which meant that I became very skilled in killing. The military is only about killing. It is not about defense. It is about offense.

In my training, I learned to dehumanize the enemy, and in the process, I became dehumanized. I remember a huge drill sergeant standing in my face screaming obscenities, taking out his penis and urinating on me. There was nothing I could do because I did not know I could do anything. And I was unaware at the time how deeply those kinds of actions affect human beings. Experiences like that never go away.

My job in Vietnam was to crew helicopter gunships. Before my eighteenth birthday I had been responsible for the deaths of hundreds of people. But this was not my first experience of war. There was the war before the war, and the war after the war, and the war that continues to rage on a daily basis all over the world. My life in high school was one form of war; my family was another form of war. I was prepared to kill before I killed, because I was so filled with anger, resentment, hurt, despair, and suffering. And my story is not unusual. There are similar stories every day all over the world. There will never be peace on Earth until we have peace within ourselves. We have to be able to look deeply into the nature of our suffering—to touch, embrace, and hold it—before we can touch peace.

In 1967, when I was shot down for the fifth time, the pilot and the aircraft commander were killed and the gunner was critically wounded. As I lay pinned in the overturned helicopter, I could smell the fuel leaking, and I could hear the gunfire hitting the helicopter. I was convinced I would die and believed that I *should* die. I did not want to survive, because I hated myself and what I had done. But I did not die. I was hospitalized for nine months, and at the age of twenty I was discharged from the military.

On my way home, as I walked across the airport in Newark to change planes—a highly decorated soldier in uniform—I was approached by a very attractive young woman. I thought she was interested in me or wanted to talk, but when she got within inches of my face, she spat on me. I went to a bar and got drunk, and

I stayed drunk and high for the next fifteen years. I needed intoxicants because I had no skills or ability to touch the depth of suffering in my life. By not being able to embrace my suffering, I could not transform it, and it leaked out in indirect ways. My life was full of anger, rage, and violence; it was the only way I knew to be.

I have no idea how or when things began to turn around for me. In 1990, I shut myself in my house, afraid to leave, no longer able to touch society because of all that it represented for me. When I walked outside and heard jets flying overhead, I cringed because I could see tree lines going up in napalm and young Vietnamese running from villages. When I walked into the grocery store, I could not take a can of vegetables off the shelf because I was afraid it was booby-trapped. The feelings were vivid, but this time I did not run away. I knew that in order for it to be transformed, I had to stay with my reality.

I heard about Thich Nhat Hanh from a social worker in Cambridge, Massachusetts, who told me about a Zen monk who had some success helping Vietnam veterans to heal. She did not say that he was Vietnamese. Six months later, someone else told me about a retreat for Vietnam veterans run by this same man. I telephoned the retreat center, not because I wanted to, but because nothing in my life was working and I did not know what else to do. I wanted my life to be different. So, terrified, I went to the retreat.

In Vietnam I had learned ways to deny terror and to just go forward. This is what got me to the retreat. But when this Vietnamese monk walked into the room and sat down, and I looked into his face, I started to cry. I realized in the moment of his sitting there that I did not know the Vietnamese people in any other way than as the enemy. They were the enemy and if they were the enemy then I did not know how to relate to anyone else in the world other than as the enemy. Everyone was the enemy.

One of the first things this monk said was, "You veterans are the light at the tip of the candle. You burn hot. You have the ability through your experience to help in the transformation of the world, to transform the violence, to transform the hate, to transform the despair. You need to talk." And he said, "The non-veterans need to listen. The veterans deserve to be understood. To understand someone you need to place yourself in his skin."

All my life, when I tried to talk about these things, people always went away. They said, "You're too intense. I can't deal with you. I've got to leave." I have come to understand that what they were really saying was, "In relationship with you, I am touching parts of myself that I do not want to touch."

Thich Nhat Hanh said that the non-veterans were more responsible for the war than the veterans, and I knew the truth in that. He was articulating things I had known all my life. Since the end of the war, thousands of Vietnam vets, young men and women, have killed themselves. I can be sure that there are one or two veterans in every group of homeless people I see on the street, and many have ended up in prisons. We have been marginalized.

I did not know what to do. I approached Sister Chân Không after the retreat. I wanted to make amends for the killing, but I did not have the courage to say that. All I said was, "I would really like to go back to Vietnam."

And she smiled. "You need to come to Plum Village first. Let us help you." (Plum Village is Thich Nhat Hanh's retreat center in France.)

I said, "I cannot afford to come."

She said, "We will buy your ticket." This was my enemy. No one in this country had ever offered me an opportunity like that to heal.

During the summer in Plum Village, a community of Vietnamese people lives in the Lower Hamlet. When I arrived, Sister Chân Không told me that that's where I was to live. So there I was in a community of 400 Vietnamese, and every place I turned, another terrifying memory would come up from the war. I could not work hard enough, I could not keep busy enough to get away from those memories. When I wanted to talk to somebody, I would approach a monk or a nun and try to explain what was going on, saying, "I see the young Vietnamese women in their *ao-dai* coming into the *zendo*, and I remember a gun run in a village where I was responsible for killing thirty or forty people."

When I would start to talk like that, the monks and nuns would say, "The past is in the past. There is only the present moment, and it is beautiful."

I did not know how to deal with that. So I did not say anything until one day when I began to talk about the war and a monk gave me the same spiel, and I turned around in real anger and said, "The past is not in the past for me. It is in the present moment and it is ugly."

I talked to Sister Chân Không about this and she said, "If you are living intensely in the present moment, the past and the future are also there. You just need to be with them like still water." That was all I needed.

I went back to Plum Village the following year and have since returned twice. Each visit I have to confront myself over and over again. I was victimized, but I cannot continue to maintain the posture of being a victim. I need to heal. I need to transform. I need to challenge the ideas that I have been subjected to throughout my life.

Thich Nhat Hanh always teaches the Five Buddhist Precepts. The first is: "Aware of the suffering caused by the destruction of life, I vow to cultivate compassion and to learn the ways of protecting the lives of people, animals, plants, and minerals. I am determined not to kill, not to let others kill, and not to condone any act of killing in my thinking and way of life." For me this is a lifelong practice, and it begins with getting in close touch with the feelings in me and working moment by moment to embrace them and to transform them into love and understanding.

Claude Thomas is a combat veteran of the Vietnam War and a writer who helps lead meditation retreats for veterans and others. This story was excerpted from *A Joyful Path: Community, Transformation, and Peace* by Thich Nhat Hanh and friends.

Love in the Here and Now

JOANNA CAMPBELL SLAN

The thick cables strained, a low whine filled the air, and our elevator car lurched. Holding my son in my arms, I widened my stance to keep from falling. Unblinkingly, we looked up. We were climbing the Eiffel Tower, as one slow turn of the giant winch hauled us up into the clouds of Paris.

Across from me, the old woman scowled. Her expensive trenchcoat was buttoned up to her sagging throat, and a glorious shawl was pinned over one shoulder. In her manicured hands she held an Aigner purse, and she shifted herself wearily against the open grid of the elevator car, adjusting her weight against the carved head of a mahogany walking cane.

I had first noticed her in the Jules Verne Restaurant, where we had eaten our lunch. How out of the place we seemed! The legendary cuisine of the Jules Verne had attracted my husband and me—and since were traveling *en famille*, we came with our two-year-old son as well. We savored each dish while juggling our busy tyke, in a dining room filled with elegant travelers from all over the globe. A phalanx of waiters, looking curiously like penguins in their tuxedos, retrieved tossed spoons and dirtied napkins as we struggled with our child at the table.

Alas! My fantasy had been to dine with my husband alone, here on the first-floor landing of the Eiffel Tower in my best black dress, and to sip champagne through the evening, and then to end the night with a romantic toasting to the sleeping City of Light. But finances and child care had not cooperated, and so I parted with fantasy and stood here, with reality, holding an active little boy and shrinking under the glare of an annoyed matron. Certainly, our frivolity had ruined her lunch. Obviously, our youth seemed inappropriate. She must be raging inside about ugly Americans.

"How old is he?" Her gaze centered on my squirming son.

I was startled. Her voice was low and smoldering with a cultured European accent.

"He is twenty-eight months old."

She grunted and turned her head to view the plaza below us. Then she turned and lifted her cane to point at my child.

"Don't let him forget this day." She paused. "Some of us wait too long. My husband and I always said we'd come to Paris. But first it was the children. Then it was the business, and now..."

I leaned toward her. "Now?"

Her sagging eyes locked onto my son's. Hers were a faint shade of blue, like blueberry stains in a sink. His were as green and crisp as the grass below us.

"Now, he is gone and I am here alone."

My husband shifted and pulled me close to him. My son giggled in delight.

"It is...hard to enjoy such beauty...alone." She sighed and wiped the back of her hand across her eyes as a small child would. Then she looked away.

So my trip was not a fantasy. I live, here, in reality. Love can't always wait for moonlit nights, sparkling wine, and romantic interludes. Even in the City of Light. It is here and now. Lest we wait too long.

Joanna Campbell Slan is the author of seven scrapbooking books including *The Best of British Scrapbooking and Cardmaking,* the first international book on the topic. She is a contributor to many of the *Chicken Soup for the Soul* books and books in the *Chocolate for a Woman's Soul* series. Her textbook *Using Stories and Humor: Grab Your Audience* is used by instructors all over the globe. An award-winning speaker and an international presenter, she and her husband David live in a suburb of St. Louis with their teenager, Michael. You can learn more about her work at www.scrapbookstorytelling.com.

The Murderer

ALBERT TOMEI

Throughout his criminal trial, the defendant's deadly stare never varied. It was his beacon of hate, warning everyone to stay away.

If the eyes are the window to the soul, the defendant's soul was in the firm grasp of Beelzebub.

The young man in my courtroom in Brooklyn was charged, along with two cohorts, with gunning down another young man execution-style. The defendant was no stranger to the system, and when the jury returned a verdict of guilty, it seemed as if his deadly gaze only increased in intensity.

Every day for two weeks, the victim's family attended the court sessions. On the day of sentencing, his mother and grandmother addressed the court.

Ordinarily, when the victim's kin speak at sentencing, they choose not to speak to the defendant directly. On those occasions when they do, they usually express in virulent terms their repulsion of the defendant and his deed.

When this victim's mother approached the assistant district attorney's table, she turned slowly toward the convicted killer.

Looking into his hateful stare, she began to speak in muted tones. There was no primal call for revenge or retribution. Instead her message was distilled by days of endless grief. "I have no bad feelings," she said. "I could never hate you."

For the first time since the trial began, the defendant's eyes lost their laser force and appeared to surrender to a life force that only a mother can generate: nurturing, unconditional love.

Following the brokenhearted mother, the grandmother also looked directly into the defendant's eyes and spoke unflinchingly about her loss.

She told him she was sorry he had committed the crime because "you're a nice-looking man." Her message was simple and clear.

"So you did the crime and I am sorry you've got to do the time. You broke the golden rule: loving God with all your heart, soul, and mind. You broke the law: loving your neighbor as yourself. I am your neighbor.

"So anyway," she continued, "you have my address. You want to write, I'll write you back, because I sat here for two weeks and for sixteen months I tried to hate you. But you know what? I could not hate you. I feel sorry for you because you made a wrong choice."

After the grandmother finished, I looked at the defendant.

His head was hanging low. There was no more swagger, no more stare.

The destructive and evil forces within him collapsed helplessly before this remarkable display of humaneness.

In light of all that preceded it, the sentence I imposed—thirty-seven years to life in prison—seemed insignificant.

Albert Tomei is a justice of the New York State Supreme Court.

Bridehood Revisited

CHLOE WOODLAND

Yesterday my husband entered his first race: the Stuffed Turkey Race, five miles, no big deal. He came in eightieth in a field of one hundred runners. As he said later, the lame and the halt, the blind and the aged beat him. And as I stood there in the cold wind, waiting for him to come around the curve toward the finish line, I learned something, again, about love.

So many times, I've been struck by the disparity between the love that moves us toward marriage and the love that evolves over the years that keeps a marriage going. I probably married Elliot Strauss because he was the handsomest man who wanted to marry me when I was ready, at thirty, to embark on a second marriage. The sexual chemistry was very strong. I suppose I should also give myself credit for having known at the time that he was funny, smart, not given to physical or emotional violence, and politically liberal. The rest was blind luck.

Over the eighteen years we've been together, however, there have been plenty of times when I haven't felt so lucky. I have a rampant shadow side that is actively anti-relationship. When the dark side has been dominant I have hated my husband, made long lists of his shortcomings, and engaged in endless inner monologues about his flaws. I have brooded about how much nobler, more creative, wealthier, more traveled, urbane, rural, translucent, opaque, etcetera, my life would have been if only I had attached myself to a different kind of man. I've dreamt of escaping to Uruguay to wait tables at a bar near a tropical river. A lot of this has to do with my own psychopathology and, of course, some of it must have to do with who he is. I am not anyone's idea of perfection and neither is he. We have serious flaws. There have been bitter times when we've spoken of divorce, and there have been sweet times. We have muddled along.

Over the last month, Elliot's father, Abe, has been slowly dying of congestive heart failure, in several different rooms in two different hospitals. It has been nightmarish. My mother-in-law has been a warrior, fighting the bureaucracy of a huge city hospital to get clear answers, alternatives, humane treatment. And my husband has been at his father's bedside every day, telling stories, making him laugh, playing a Sonny Terry and Brownie McGhee CD for him, walking him and his IV cart slowly around the cardiac-care unit when Abe could walk. Rubbing his back.

I don't think I have ever loved him so much as a few days ago, at the end of a miserable, claustrophobic day by his father's side. Abe's foot started to cramp and Elliot knelt on the floor by his bed massaging it. Abe wanted to press his foot against the floor, but wasn't able to stand, so Elliot placed his father's foot against his chest.

"Just press against me, Dad. I'm strong. I'm not going any-where."

How many times have I pressed against him to find him strong. While I, the practiced escape artist, have indulged in fantasies of flight, have tortured him with those fantasies, he has been there, unwavering. I wish I could say that I knew when I married him seventeen years ago that I had a sense of the profounder depths of love, that I knew the value of loyalty, fidelity, steadfast commitment over the long run. When we were married in Berkeley, we eschewed the old-fashioned vows of sickness and health, richer or poorer, till death do us part. It is now, in the presence of the aching and enormous love between Abe and Irene, that argumentative old couple—watching them kiss good-bye (for the last time?) as she prepares to leave him each night in the hospital—that I feel the depth of those tired old phrases.

As I was standing around by myself at the Stuffed Turkey Race, waiting for the runners to finish, I noticed a lively family, exuberant with health and chatty bonhomie. Everyone, even the grandfather, was tall, athletic, and good-looking, as if they had walked out of the pages of an L.L. Bean catalogue, and I did my usual trick of imagining lives that were somehow better than mine. Their runner came in long before mine did.

But when my balding, forty-eight-year-old racer finally rounded the bend, limping slightly because his hip hurt him, I felt such pride that my eyes welled with tears as I clapped my mittened hands. I realized: In this crowd, only I know the true measure of this man. Here is a winner, someone to stick with for the long run. He can press against me. I'm not going anywhere.

Chloe Woodland is a writer and photographer living in Dobbs Ferry, New York.

Forgiveness

MARK GRUBER, O.S.B.

My grandfather is ninety-nine years old. He is in very good health now. He bowls quite well. He drives, and just got his driver's license renewed for four years! His life was a difficult life.

When he was four years old, before the turn of the twentieth century, he woke upon on his parents' farm one morning to discover that his father and his elder brother were missing. They had disappeared in the night.

His brother was older than he was by ten years. He was confused as to what their absence meant—disoriented. And because he was so young, his family didn't explain to him very much about what was happening.

His confusion turned to sorrow because he missed his father and his brother. But as the weeks passed, his sorrow took on a bitter tone because he began to feel rejected and abandoned.

The years passed and my grandfather had to leave school early. He was a bright boy, but at fourth grade he had to drop out to take care of his mother and his sisters and his grandmother—his mother's mother—who was living with them at the farm. He had to do the work of an adult at the age of ten, and he was stuck on that farm into his mid-twenties taking care of them.

And so his sense of being abandoned and rejected became anger and then resentment.

He began to harbor in his heart a terrible grudge against his father and against his brother.

His mother died young and he blamed it on them.

He went to the First War in Europe and he told me that he stayed on the front whenever he had a choice—whenever he could relieve somebody. He stayed in the trenches on the front lines because it didn't matter to him to live or to die, he was so filled with darkness.

He came home after the war and he married.

My mother tells me that growing up she was never allowed to ask about her grandfather; she was never allowed to ask about her uncle; they were names which were forbidden in that house.

During all this time my grandfather suffered from excruciating headaches. He had to stay home at least one day a week from the railroad or from the mill. He couldn't work. And all of this time he never spoke about his father or his brother. This condition endured until my grandfather was about seventy-five years old.

When he was seventy-five, he visited his sisters in Erie, Pennsylvania. They had a little reunion around the dinner table. And while they were talking at the dinner table, his elder sisters began reminiscing about the old days, as the old often do. And they remembered fondly the farm, and they even broached the very delicate topic of the father and the brother.

One of them said, "Too bad we didn't take the tickets."

"What tickets?" my grandfather asked.

"You know, the tickets that he sent—the tickets from the new farm."

"What new farm?" my grandfather asked.

"The new farm in California. You know, when he disappeared. Two weeks later we got tickets in the mail. He had bought land in California and he was sending for us to come."

"I didn't know about that," Grandfather said. "Why didn't you tell me?"

"Oh, you were so young. I guess we didn't think you would understand."

"Why didn't we go?"

"Well, he sent tickets for all of the daughters and for you and for mother, but not for mother's mother who was living with us. So she made the decision that she was going to stay here with her mother rather than to join her husband someplace else."

Well, this revelation struck my grandfather with great force.

All of these years he had simply felt rejected, abandoned. All of these years he had nursed in his heart hatred.

And now he realized that he was not the victim of hatred or rejection; he was the victim of…a complex family.

All of us have been victims of complex families.

And so he said to his sisters right there at the table, "I'm going to find my brother."

They laughed. He had been missing for over seventy years. "We don't know where he is; he may well be dead. You'll never find him."

He got up from the table and began to search: church registries, post office boxes, telephone books. He called lawyers. And finally after four years of searching, he found his brother in Orlando, Florida.

As soon as he found him, he bought airline tickets. The tickets they should have taken on the railroad long ago, he bought for the airplane seventy-five years later for his sisters and for himself. And they all flew to Orlando, where, by every account, there was a tearful reunion and a reconciliation.

My great-uncle was 90 years old at the time; he lived to be 101. Every year my grandfather went down there for Christmas. Every summer, my great uncle came up from Florida for all of those ten years following. They became brothers again; they renewed their friendship, filled in the gaps as best they could.

My grandfather's headaches stopped altogether.

I was ordained during that time. And at the time of my ordination, my grandfather pulled me aside—never a very outspoken man. He said this to me: "Wherever you go, make sure you tell people not to wait forever to forgive. Make sure you tell them to let go as soon as they can. I waited a whole lifetime; I was dead for more than seventy years, but God was merciful to me, and now I am alive."

We are all called to let things go.

Father Mark Gruber also contributed "The Butterfly Man" to this collection.

The Physics of Kindness

Huey D. Johnson

Acts of kindness have a way of coming home again. An elderly man, living alone in a cheap Miami hotel room, recently experienced this phenomenon.

Forty years ago, that man appealed to his twenty-three-year-old sign-painting partner to go back to school and study physics. Hanging in space from a scaffold, painting billboards, helps people get to know each other. This man felt his young friend and colleague had a remarkable talent to understand and explain the natural wonders. Inspired by his older mentor, the young man left sign painting to seek an education.

Paul Hewitt was that young person, and he is now a nationally famous, San Francisco-based author and former physics teacher at San Francisco City College. His accomplishments include writing *Conceptual Physics*, the best-selling college physics text in America for the last twenty-five years. More importantly, he is a great pioneering teacher. His students have been inspired and become successful, and while there are more stories about Hewitt, this one is an important, human part of him.

Paul became my friend in graduate school. I urged him to come to San Francisco, the place where I wanted to live. And though he was offered other jobs, including one from Dr. Teller's bomb factory, Paul wanted to teach physics to students from a working-class background similar to his own. He could accomplish that by teaching at City College. His popularity there was unparalleled. Hundreds of students registered for his introductory physics class each semester.

Paul's interest in physics included a love of the subject and the working mysteries of it. The phenomenon of forces and physical factors that make up all things is a subject that too few know about. He felt that the popular approach of emphasizing mathematical computations turned off a large number of students whose lives would be enhanced by a knowledge of physics, whatever their profession. Hewitt sees physics equations as guides to thinking that show nature's connections rather than recipes for calculations.

Hewitt, now retired from teaching at San Francisco City College, always started the first lecture by telling the origins of his interest in physics. He talks of how that elderly sign-painting partner inspired him years go. Finding and thanking his mentor was an unfinished task.

Recently a student raised his hand and asked, "Did you ever thank the guy?" Paul replied that he had lost track of him and had not been able to locate him since. The student happened to have experience using a computer to trace people. At the next class, the student handed Paul an address and phone number for a cheap Miami hotel.

Paul penned a note of thanks, described his successful career, and enclosed a $10,000 check in appreciation, which needless to say, came as an overwhelming surprise to the recipient. He used the gift to fly to San Francisco. The popularity of Paul's textbook over the years has made Paul financially comfortable, and he owns a large home on a lagoon in Hawaii. Rather than let his friend return to Miami, Paul suggested that he become the caretaker of his Hawaii home—with a salary and free board. He accepted.

And there the old friend lives today, a happy transplant from Miami. Within a month, while walking on the beach, the new caretaker met a woman and they fell in love. That was his first date in twenty years—all because many years earlier he encouraged a friend to develop an inherent ability to teach and inspire students.

Huey D. Johnson was a columnist with the *San Francisco Examiner*, a former secretary of the California Resources Agency, and is the founder and current head of the Resource Renewal Institute of San Francisco.

Big Howie

Donald G. Smith

I hadn't thought of Big Howie in years. He was an outsized lout who moved into our neighborhood when I was in the fifth grade, and he seemed to disappear about a year later.

The first few months with Big Howie were sheer hell. He was about a year older than the rest of us, big for his age, and about as mean a person as I ever knew.

He looked upon fifth grade as his person fiefdom, taking whatever he wanted and striking down dissenters with savage intensity. Anyone who dared report these practices to a school authority was in for unspeakable retaliation; and none of us had the courage to break the code of silence.

Big Howie's reign of terror ended abruptly one spring day when he got into an altercation with a small, bespectacled boy named Fritz. The source of the trouble was a Milky Way candy bar. Howie demanded that Fritz give it to him; Fritz refused, and Howie took it anyway, giving Fritz some whacks on the head for his bad attitude.

Well, Fritz had an older brother in high school; big, strong, and extremely protective of his younger brothers and sisters. I don't know how he got the word so fast, but big brother came to school that very day.

He took Howie behind the manual training room and settled the problem with minimum discussion, not only for Fritz, but for all of us. Big Howie, bloody and humiliated, stopped being a bully.

I remembered this incident a few weeks ago while listening to an overeducated mealy-mouth who was a guest on a talk radio show. He was expounding on the old "violence-never-settled-anything" theme, interspersed with a meaningful dialogue or two, and I suddenly saw the vision of an ex-bully facing his peers in the fifth grade, while bleeding from the nose, mouth, and both eyes.

Violence had indeed settled something that day—quickly, decisively.

I do not advocate violence as a primary means of settling disputes, but I drift away from the let's-talk-it-over crowd in my refusal to discount it completely as a problem-solving tool. There is a place for violence in our society, and that place is when no other alternative is offered.

There is no other way that the careers of, say, an Adolf Hitler or a John Dillinger could have been terminated. Neither man showed much inclination to "talk things over," and it is highly questionable that the tweed-and-pipe set could have evoked much in the way of a meaningful dialogue from either of them.

In fact, the world would have benefited immeasurably if both of them would have checked out, violently if necessary, much earlier than they did. They could have taken Joe Stalin and Al Capone with them, and there wouldn't have been many tears shed.

In the case of Big Howie, it is possible that someone eventually could have reached him with the message that bringing pain to smaller, weaker people wasn't the right way to go.

Sure it was an unpleasant experience for Howie, but think of how much grief it saved the rest of us.

As a very wise man once said: "Better him than me."

Donald G. Smith, a retired editor of corporate publications, is a freelance writer living in Santa Maria, California.

Kurt's View

KURT VONNEGUT WITH DAVID H. FREEDMAN

On employment: I believe half of the duty of every inventor is to make a product that is better and cheaper, and the other half is to create a job that is more satisfying. We do only half of it. People are never mentioned, as though they don't figure in the equation at all. Technocrats don't give a damn about anything but the machines. They're rational enough to know that there is no afterlife, and so they settle for the benefits they can get now, and they don't care what happens to the world afterwards.

We're always trying to replace jobs. Keeping lists, taking inventory, those are all things to do with life. And then somebody comes along and says, "Hey, you don't need to do that anymore." Well, thanks, but how the hell am I supposed to support my family? You, you silly fool, you've still got a job, sure. There's this great word that the British use all the time: *redundant*. Workers are declared redundant. How'd you like to come into this world and be told you're redundant? Built into human beings is a need, which nobody bothers to even acknowledge, to do something useful. But instead of worrying about what human beings need, we worry about what machines need. There's no talk at all about what human beings are deprived of; all the talk is about what industries are being deprived of.

There's all this talk about building the information superhighway and new networks. But there's never talk about what's happening to this network [taps the side of his head], which is already in place. There's utter indifference to it. Christ, I can remember when TV was going to teach my children Korean and trigonometry. Rural areas wouldn't even have to have very well educated teachers; all they'd have to do is turn on the box. Well, we can see what TV really did. Look at what the O. J. Simpson trial has done to everyone. So much for all those Tom Swifts talking about the enormous benefit of what they were doing. The information superhighway will be two lanes loaded with tollgates, and it's going to tell you what to look for. People will just watch the show.

We are not born with imagination. It has to be developed by teachers, by parents. There was a time when imagination was very important because it was the major source of entertainment. In 1892 if you were a seven-year-old, you'd read a story—just a very simple one—about a girl whose dog had died. Doesn't that make you want to cry? Don't you know how that little girl feels? And you'd read another story about a rich man slipping on a banana peel. Doesn't that make you want to laugh? And this imagination circuit is being built in your head. If you go to an art gallery, here's just a square with daubs of paint on it that haven't moved in hundreds of years. No sound comes out of it.

The imagination circuit is taught to respond to the most minimal of cues. A book is an arrangement of 26 phonetic symbols, 10 numbers, and about 8 punctuation marks, and people can cast their eyes over these and envision the eruption of Mount Vesuvius or the Battle of Waterloo. But it's no longer necessary for teachers and parents to build these circuits. Now there are professionally produced shows with great actors, very convincing sets, sound, music. And now there's the information highway. We don't need the circuits any more than we need to know how to ride horses. Those of us who had imagination circuits built can look in someone's face and see stories there; to everyone else, a face will just be a face.

I work at home, and if I wanted to, I could have a computer right by my bed, and I'd never have to leave it. But I use a typewriter, and afterwards I mark up the pages with a pencil. Then I call up this woman named Carol out in Woodstock and say, "Are you still doing typing?" Sure she is, and her husband is trying to track bluebirds out there and not having much luck, and so we chitchat back and forth, and I say, "O.K., I'll send you the pages."

Then I'm going down the steps, and my wife calls up, "Where are you going?" I say, "Well, I'm going to go buy an envelope." And she says, "You're not a poor man. Why don't you buy a thousand envelopes? They'll deliver them, and you can put them in a closet." And I say, "Hush." So I go down the steps here, and I go out to this newsstand across the street where they sell magazines and lottery tickets and stationery. I have to get in line because there are people buying candy and all that sort of thing, and I talk to them. The woman behind the counter has a jewel between her eyes, and when it's my turn, I ask her if there have been any big winners lately. I get my envelope and seal it up and go to the postal convenience center down the block at the corner of 47th Street and 2nd Avenue, where I'm secretly in love with the woman behind the counter. I keep absolutely poker-faced; I never let her know how I feel about her. One time I had my pocket picked in there and got to meet a cop and tell him about it. Anyway, I address the envelope to Carol in Woodstock. I stamp the envelope and mail it in a mailbox in front of the post office, and I go home. And I've had a hell of a good time. And I tell you, we are here on Earth to fart around, and don't let anybody tell you any different.

Kurt Vonnegut, master of contemporary American literature, was born on Armistice Day (November 11), 1922, in Indianapolis, Indiana. He started writing in high school, served in the U.S. Army, became a German prisoner of war during the Battle of the Bulge, and survived the firebombing of Dresden in February 1945. Since then he has written many acclaimed essays, short stories, and books, including *The Sirens of Titan*, *Cat's Cradle*, and *Slaughterhouse-Five*. He lives in New York City.

No Statute of Limitations

RACHEL NAOMI REMEN, M.D.

Yitzak was a survivor. Liberated from a concentration camp in 1945, he had come to America, worked and studied hard, and was now a respected research physicist. His first words endeared him to me. His Slavic accent reminded me of some of the older people in my own family. Two years before, he had been diagnosed with cancer. Now he had come to our retreat for people with cancer to see if he would engage and possibly defeat this enemy with the power of his mind, the aspect of his being he trusted most profoundly.

At Commonweal we touch people a great deal more than was his custom. Disconcerted at first, he would ask, "Is all dis, all dis huggy-huggy? Vat is dis luff the strangers? Vat is dis?" But he let us hug him anyway. After a while he began to hug us back.

The Commonweal retreats last for a week. By the fourth day the inner silence, which has been slowly generated by the daily yoga practice, has become very deep, and spontaneous insights often arise. Sometimes this silence allows people to find their own truth for the first time.

On the fourth day, in the meditation which begins the morning session, Yitzak had an experience. It seemed to him that through his closed lids he would see a deep pinkish light, very beautiful and tender. Startled, he realized this light surrounded him and came in some mysterious fashion from his chest. When he told us about it later, he said it was like being inside of a big rose: very touching, because his last name means "little rose" in Polish.

In the moment, however, he became frightened. He was aware that the light had a direction, it was pouring out of his chest "like a big hemorrhage." It seemed to be coming from his heart and it made him feel vulnerable.

Yitzak had survived the concentration camps. For many years he had lived, as it were, in a world of strangers. A deeply loving person, since his experience as a boy, he had been very cautious with respect to his heart, loving only close people, only family. This way of living had helped him feel safer, had worked for him until now. But there is often fear behind such a wary lifestyle and now for the first time he had begun to feel some of this. It was uncomfortable for him.

The retreat staff dealt with his discomfort in the way they deal with everything else; they did not try to fix it, to explain away his experience, or to interpret it for him. Instead they listened with interest and continued to support him as he tried to work out its meaning for himself. Over the next few days he seemed to relax more, to become more open.

Sunday, in the last session of the retreat, I try to tie up the loose ends. I knew Yitzak had been troubled by his experience, so I asked him how things were. He laughed. "Better," he said, and began to tell us of a walk he had taken on the beach the day before. In his mind, he had talked to God, asking God what all this was about, and had received comfort. Touched, I asked him what God had to say. He laughed again. "An, Rachel-le, I say to Him, 'God is it O.K. to luff strangers?' And God says, 'Yitzak, vat is dis *strangers*? *You* make strangers. *I* don't make strangers.'"

There is no statute of limitations on healing. Forty years ago because of his life experiences, Yitzak had closed his heart. Now as he sought a way to heal his body, he had begun to heal in other ways as well. In the struggle to survive our wounds, we may adapt a strategy of living which gets us through. Life-threatening illness may cause us to re-examine the very premises on which we have based our lives, perhaps freeing ourselves to live more fully for the first time.

Rachel Naomi Remen, M.D. also contributed "The Container" to this collection.

The Chair

JEFFREY BURKE

oon after we moved into the lighthouse station, I learned the first rule of island living: there is always a use for everything. Here there are no shopping malls or hardware stores, no telephones or mail carriers, no delivery vans to materialize through the fog with a coil of rope or a pound of nails. Every piece of old machinery and every length of rusty pipe must be saved and cherished, for at any moment some archaic remnant may be called upon to save the day.

One of my first tasks was to organize the junk in the barn and the boathouse. It took days to sort through the sea chests and wooden crates. I glued broken balusters and returned them to the front porch, refinished interior doors and hung them, patched cistern downspouts and wired them in place so rainwater once again flowed from the roof to the brick reservoir in the cellar.

Not everything I found was hard and mechanical. Some of the old furniture was a softer, more soulful reminder of the past: a side chair with a rose embroidered on its worn cushion. An iron bed with a sagging mattress, dressers whose drawers were filled with creased photographs and old diaries. Heaps of the old furniture were everywhere, disjointed and scarred, with broken spindles jutting from the piles like bleached ribs in an elephant graveyard. My son Peter and I spent weeks gluing, sanding, and painting. Finally, one by one, the rooms began to blossom, each one attracting a perfect combination of freshly painted pieces. Every item found its proper place, its intended use.

Except for one. It was a rocker upholstered in brown vinyl. Old, maybe fifty years or more. Squarish. Rigid. And ugly, just plain ugly. Paint and polish could help it no more than the cosmetics of an undertaker primping a corpse for burial. Its pointed rockers jutted up at an angle designed to gash the shins of those who strayed too close, and its plastic upholstery was the color of Maine mud in late March. Torn badly on one side, the fake leather gaped like a horrid wound, exposing swaths of stuffing that appeared to be decaying hair from some prehistoric beast. Although ripped and tattered, the material showed none of the wear patterns usually found on old furniture; apparently, no one had ever sat on it! Like a feared leper, the chair must have been locked away in dusty attics for its entire life.

I tried to find a place for it, I really did. I tried it in every room of the house, on the porch and even in the kitchen. But in each place I tried, its vile nature seemed only to grow, as if the chair were taking a life of its own. It threatened the ambiance of our fledgling inn, the safety of our guests, and our budding reputation as fine innkeepers. It would have to go.

I posted a notice in the Island Store:

> FREE: NICE ROCKING CHAIR
> SEE IT AT THE LIGHTHOUSE

Several families scheduled interviews. I waited nervously while my wife Judi baked blueberry muffins and brewed a pot of her favorite Colombian-Sumatran blend.

Leland Small was the first to arrive. On his way back into the harbor from hauling lobster traps, he dropped anchor and skiffed ashore. I had the chair sitting there just inside the boathouse door, its rockers polished, its vinyl skin waxed and gleaming in the bright July sunshine. The torn side faced the wall, and I made sure the most glaring deformity wouldn't be noticed: a strip of duct tape bound the wound and kept the innards from spilling out.

Lee greeted me, then paced back and forth in front of the chair, eyeing it uncomfortably. He twisted the ends of his coarse red mustache, searching for the right words. A gentle fellow, he finally built up the courage to deliver the verdict.

"Well, Jeff, I just need something for the shop, where I can sit and knit bait bags and such—nothing fancy, of course—but to tell you the truth, that's got to be the ugliest damn chair I've ever seen!"

"Well, yes, it doesn't look like a very good chair," I admitted. "But this here chair is unique. You could use it for lots of things: rocking Mary's baby to sleep, a sawbuck for holding lobster traps while your repair them. How about kindling for stoking your stoves?"

"Nope," said Lee. "That chair reeks of trouble: I wouldn't even set my chainsaw down on that dreadful thing!"

He didn't wait for the muffins and coffee. He was so eager to get away he almost forgot to loop his skiff's painter around the stern cleat. As he pulled free of the rocks, he glanced back suspiciously, as if he expected to see me hefting the cursed chair down through the ledges in an attempt to toss it aboard.

Several other folks came to look at the chair, but the results were always the same (it doesn't take long for the word to get around). After that, of course, there were no more interested parties. A few curious kids from the village did come to gawk, as if it were some deformed creature in a circus sideshow.

I was getting desperate. Memories of our years in Pemaquid came to mind: I remembered our Nubian goat, Florence. She broke a leg one winter and I had to ask my brother to put the poor thing down. Now again, I asked a few of my new island friends to take this albatross off my hands, pleading for help with a quandary I couldn't solve alone. But they only smiled, snickered, found ways to avoid me.

I paced the boathouse, glaring at the chair. Drastic measures were needed.

Fire! A fine choice! I could gore the vinyl with a broken oar and fling the rocker into a blazing brush pile. But the burning vinyl might give off black noxious smoke, polluting the atmosphere and calling attention to my failure to find a use for the chair. That would never do.

Drowning was another possibility. I could weigh it down with chimney blocks, drag it down to the shore on a moonless night, and dump it overboard. But with my luck a scallop dragger would haul it up and toss it back on our shore: after all, by now the entire world knew where the ugliest chair in Maine belonged.

I could bury it alive—that would be a kick! It would be difficult, though: around the lighthouse there is no soil, only granite boulders and volcanic ledge. It's easy digging in the gravel pit, but getting the awkward chair over to the east side without being seen would be tricky. And even if I succeeded, chances are that sooner or later someone excavating for sand would come upon the remains. There would be no doubt who the culprit was.

Since none of the traditional techniques would do, something more creative was needed, I thought, leaning against the workbench and glaring at the chair. I could tie a pair of deer antlers on the chair and hide it in the woods near the shore; doubtless there would be a boat of poachers in the fall who would spot the horns and blow the dastardly thing to smithereens. Or perhaps I could lash an outboard motor to the back and send it skating across the water on its ski-like rockers, to meet its fate running aground on some distant ledge—or being eaten by sharks! But with all its high-tech equipment, the Coast Guard would probably come to its rescue and the media would pick up the story:

COAST GUARD CAPTURES
HIGH-SPEED VINYL CHAIR

Once photos were released, the chair would be instantly identified and I would be apprehended.

PHANTOM CHAIR TRACED TO ISLAND—
INNKEEPER CHARGED WITH FAILURE
TO FIND USE FOR PERFECTLY GOOD ITEM

I would appeal, of course. But my career would be ruined and I would be forced to sell the station to cover legal expenses. There would be nothing left to live for, everything I worked so hard for all these years lost. My friends would desert me. Judi would find solace with a more successful man. Shamed to tears, the kids would turn away from me. Even Maggie would slink away the first chance she got, indignant over the sparse pickings as we bummed from town to town, sleeping in bus stations and begging handouts on street corners.

My head reeled with the consequences. I became dizzy, hot, faint. My knees began to tremble, my stomach filled with lead. The world around me became hazy, the boathouse floor began to slump, and, as I faltered, my hands groped for anything stable—and I collapsed…into…the chair.

For a few moments I lay recovering, the chair rocking gently from the impact. It had been soft enough to cushion my fall, yet solid enough not to buckle.

I waited. I felt a little better, a little stronger. The dizzying gyrations in my head began to ease. The chair cradled me in its soft lap, the way my mother did when I was a little boy, and the cushions began to absorb my anxiety. I pushed gently against the floor. The chair surged, instantaneously, like a fine racehorse reacting to its jockey's urgings. The smooth faded vinyl was warm from the afternoon sun, sensuous and alive to my touch, and the rockers creaked a pleasant lullaby that soothed my frazzled nerves. I closed my eyes and rocked.

Today that once-despised hulk of hardwood, hair, and plastic still sits by the boathouse door, positioned just right so I can gaze southwest out to Saddleback Ledge. I come here to find a moment of serenity, a taste of peace, a chance to dwell a bit with the Island Spirit. When I am here, I am never alone. My chair by the boathouse door has become my friend and confidant—and a reminder to me that there is always a use for everything, even things that are as ugly as sin.

Jeffrey Burke is a writer and the owner of the Keeper's House Inn on Isle au Haut, Maine. This story was excerpted from his book, *Island Lighthouse Inn: A Chronicle.*

Peak Experience

MARK HAWTHORNE

From the base of the hill, it looked like a long climb. I had been in Ladakh, high in the Himalayas of India, for a month when I finally visited Tsemo Gompa, a tiny, fifteenth-century monastery on Namgyal Peak overlooking Leh. "Go to the *gompa* today," Yangchen, my Ladakhi landlady, had told me. "It is an easy walk."

The path to the *gompa* was a dusty, rocky trail that countless visitors had formed for the likes of me to climb, and halfway up the hill I took a moment to enjoy the view. The city of Leh, Ladakh's capital and once part of the Silk Route, spread out from the ancient palace to a narrow ribbon of highway, with dozens of low, flat-roofed buildings in between. Barley fields in neat, asymmetrical shapes carpeted the valley floor. Punctuating the landscape were Buddhist *chortens*, their whiteness a stark contrast to the surrounding earth tones. Looking like giant chess pieces set against the barren mountain scenery, the *chortens* each house a Buddhist relic and are believed to have been first built during Emperor Ashoka's reign 200 years before Christ. I resumed my trek and turned to see a lone hiker just beginning to make the climb; I assumed it was just another curious pilgrim. But when he quickly managed to catch up with me, I knew he had to be Ladakhi. His light-brown pants and blue pullover sweater looked too clean to have come up the hill with him.

"*Julé*," I said, greeting him with the Ladakhi word for hello, goodbye, and thank you.

"*Julé*," he said. "American?"

"Yes," I answered, a bit embarrassed that it was so obvious. He balanced a set of keys in one hand and a wine bottle in the other, yet he scaled that steep trail with the skill of a mountain goat. I, in contrast, scrambled up slowly—often on my hands and knees—trying to gain purchase on the jagged earth. Within moments he and his unsullied clothes had outdistanced me.

When at last I met him at the summit, he was unlocking the monastery door. He showed me into one of the temples—a dark chamber festooned with colorful paper garlands. Sandalwood incense barely masked the musty odor of a room that was too long kept secret. An altar in the center of the room held a small *chorten*, on either side of which stood a Tantric Buddhist statue. The statues' heads and multiple arms reflected the dim light from a score of votive lamps on the floor, adding a dramatic highlight to the scene. A few green apples and a bowl of rice rested at the foot of the altar—an offering to the gods.

My guide bowed and filled the lamps with clarified butter from his wine bottle, lit the few that had burned out, and then ushered me outside. He locked the door and disappeared around the corner.

Left on my own, I wandered farther uphill to the rear of the monastery, which overlooked another valley. I was atop a peak bisecting two worlds—one a wide plateau filled with human activity and vegetation, the other a pristine valley with no man-made structures.

Long lines of Buddhist prayer flags hung from ropes tied between the *gompa* and several rocky points nearby. The small flags were made from cloth in the five holy colors: red, blue, white, green, and yellow. Each was inscribed with a prayer and hung by a devotee to disintegrate in the elements, carrying its message of peace into the winds. As I sat facing Leh under a rainbow of the wildly flapping flags, a woman and a young boy approached from the opposite side of the hill. They each tied a red, freshly printed flag over an old one that had long ago been bleached a pale pink in the Himalayan sun. They paused long enough to show their respect for the *gompa*, then retreated down the hill.

I sat and stared across the Indus Valley to the mountains. The jagged peaks, some reaching heights above 20,000 feet, are often home to ascetic monks who find the isolated locale ideal for meditation. I wondered if perhaps a monk could be sitting on a lofty perch that very moment, looking across the valley toward this sacred site.

About halfway down the hill stood Leh Palace, inspired—says the legend—by the Potala, the Dalai Lama's erstwhile winter palace in Lhasa. As I sat watching the shadow of the *gompa* stretch behind me, the rarefied air became cool and still, as if heralding a great awakening, and I was overcome by a sense of belonging— something I had never felt in any other country.

The sound of copper horns interrupted my contemplation. These long, richly decorated instruments, called *rag-dum*, are played by monks and emit a loud, haunting tone. The sound seemed to be coming from the Jo-khang Buddhist temple in Leh, where a thin column of smoke still rose. Sitting alone outside the monastery, enjoying the Himalayan scenery and the monks' music, I became overwhelmed with the peaceful spirit that permeated the land. Indeed, life itself felt dramatically richer and purposeful.

Suddenly, my focus both narrowed and widened. While I lost peripheral vision, I gained an inner perspective that was both exhilarating and startling. I felt my spirit testing the boundaries of my body, making me seem at once larger and smaller than my physical form. For an instant I understood all of life's mysteries, as though some cosmic voice was telling me simply, "It is." Oddly enough, it made perfect sense to me. I saw myself as a vital component of the universe and completely understood my place in it. In an instant I understood the realm of the afterlife, the complex dualities in physics, the common truth in all religions, and the very origins of life itself.

The moment of awakening passed all too quickly—too quickly to grasp all the answers that had echoed within me. But I was left with a lingering taste of clarity; I had retained just enough understanding to give me profound peace. Without consciously seeking it, I suddenly understood the Oneness of Everything and how, as the Hindus teach, the *Atman* (individual soul) and *Brahman* (universal soul) are actually one. I also realized I would never be able to adequately describe my sense of complete joy, serenity, and comprehension. Motionless and content, I was ready to sit there for days, forgoing food and sleep, just to feast on that feeling of wonder and excitement.

Every sense felt sharpened as I walked back to my guesthouse in neighboring Changspa. I took a renewed interest in the sights, sounds, and smells of Ladakh. Many families in the village were busily winnowing in the fields, separating the chaff from the barley grain. Before the winnowing, the crop had been spread out in a large circle and beasts of burden were guided over it, threshing the grain. I watched three family members in one of the circles, gracefully scooping up the harvested crop with large wooden forks and pitching it into the air. The breeze blew away the chaff, leaving the heavier grain to fall to Earth. Content and spiritual, they sang a prayer while working, which translates as:

Oh, pure Goddess of the Winds!
Oh, beautiful Goddess of the Winds!
Carry away the chaff!

Ongsla skyot!
Separate the chaff from the grain!
Where there is no human help,
May the gods help us!
Oh, beautiful goddess,
Ongsla skyot!

The slow song had a chant-like quality, and the strong voices, in easy rhythm with the pitching and flying barley, filled me with admiration for this culture. Everything has a purpose in Ladakh. Even singing.

And nothing is wasted. Ladakhis can little afford to allow such resources as food, water, or animal and even human waste to go unused in their delicately balanced environment. Animal dung is particularly precious, for it provides fuel for cooking and warmth. Women carry large baskets made from sticks on their backs and wander throughout their village, collecting the brown pies deposited by cows, yaks, horses, and donkeys. They pick them up with bare hands—a tactile communion with the land—and adroitly toss them into the basket. The dung is then set on stone walls at home where it dries in the sun.

Each morning I would pass a few of these tireless Ladakhis, who scanned the ground in search of fuel. *"Julé!"* they would say happily upon noticing me, proudly chucking a fresh patty over one shoulder.

"Julé!" I replied. Hello, goodbye, and thank you.

A California-based writer, Mark Hawthorne works in marketing and contributes to *Hinduism Today* and *Satya* magazines. He won the 2003 Mona Schreiber Prize for Humorous Fiction and Non-Fiction.

Salvation in a Concentration Camp

Viktor E. Frankl

In spite of all the enforced physical and mental primitiveness of the life in a concentration camp, it was possible for spiritual life to deepen. Sensitive people who were used to a rich intellectual life may have suffered much pain (they were often of a delicate constitution), but the damage to their inner selves was less. They were able to retreat from their terrible surroundings to a life of inner riches and spiritual freedom.

Only in this way can one explain the apparent paradox that some prisoners of a less hardy makeup often seemed to survive camp life better than did those of a robust nature. In order to make myself clear, I am forced to fall back on personal experience. Let me tell what happened on those early mornings when we had to march to our work site.

There were shouted commands: "Detachment, forward march! Left 2-3-4! Left 2-3-4! Left 2-3-4! Left 2-3-4! First man about, left and left, and left and left! Caps off!" These words sound in my ears even now. At the order "Caps off!" we passed the gate of the camp, and searchlights were trained upon us. Whoever did not march smartly got a kick. And worse off was the man who, because of the cold, had pulled his cap back over his ears before permission was given.

We stumbled on in the darkness, over big stones and through large puddles, along the one road leading from the camp. The accompanying guards kept shouting at us and driving us with the butts of their rifles. Anyone with very sore feet supported himself on his neighbor's arm. Hardly a word was spoken; the icy wind did not encourge talk. Hiding his mouth behind his upturned collar, the man marching next to me whispered suddenly: "If our wives could see us now! I do hope they are better off in their camps and don't know what is happening to us."

That brought thoughts of my own wife to mind. And as we stumbled on for miles, slipping on icy spots, supporting each other time and again, dragging one another up and onward, nothing was said, but we both knew: each of us was thinking of his wife. Occasionally I looked at the sky, where the stars were fading and the pink light of the morning was beginning to spread behind a dark bank of clouds. But my mind clung to my wife's image, imagining it with an uncanny acuteness. I heard her answering me, saw her smile, her frank and encouraging look. Real or not, her look was then more luminous than the sun which was beginning to rise.

A thought transfixed me: For the first time in my life I saw the truth as it is set into song by so many poets, proclaimed as the final wisdom by so many thinkers. The truth—that love is the ultimate and the highest goal to which man can aspire. Then I grasped the meaning of the greatest secret that human poetry and human thought and belief have to impart: *The salvation of man is through love and in love.* I understood how a man who has nothing left in this world still may know bliss, be it only for a brief moment, in the contemplation of his beloved. In a position of utter desolation, when man cannot express himself in positive action, when his only achievement may consist of enduring his sufferings in the right way—an honorable way—in such a position man can, through loving contemplation of the image he carries of his beloved, achieve fulfillment. For the first time in my life I was able to understand the meaning of the words, "The angels are lost in perpetual contemplation of an infinite glory."

In front of me a man stumbled and those following him fell on top of him. The guard rushed over and used his whip on them all. Thus my thoughts were interrupted for a few minutes. But soon my soul found its way back from the prisoner's existence to another world, and I resumed talk with my loved one: I asked her questions and she answered; she questioned me in return and I answered.

"Stop!" We had arrived at our work site. Everybody rushed into the dark hut in the hope of getting a fairly decent tool. Each prisoner got a spade or a pickax.

"Can't you hurry up, you pigs?" Soon we had resumed the previous day's positions in the ditch. The frozen ground cracked under the point of the pickaxes, and sparks flew. The men were silent, their brains numb.

My mind still clung to the images of my wife. A thought crossed my mind: I didn't even know if she were still alive. I knew only one thing—which I have learned well by now: Love goes very far beyond the physical person of the beloved. It finds its deepest meaning in his spiritual being, his inner self. Whether or not he is actually present, whether or not he is still alive at all, ceases somehow to be of importance.

I did not know whether my wife was alive, and I had no means of finding out (during all my prison life there was no outgoing or incoming mail); but at the moment it ceased to matter. There was no need for me to know; nothing could touch the strength of my love, my thoughts, and the image of my beloved. Had I known then that my wife was dead, I think that I would still have given myself, undisturbed by that knowledge, to the contemplation of her image, and that my mental conversation with her would have been just as vivid and just as satisfying. "Set me like a seal upon thy heart, love is as strong as death."

Viktor E. Frankl, a German psychiatrist and author, passed away in 1997. This story was excerpted from his book, *Man's Search for Meaning.*

Love at First Sight

Douglas Preston

'll never forget the first time I saw Christine. I was at a posh gallery opening, watching an art video in which a man moved a piece of black plywood around a white prison cell, when I glimpsed her across the room. I thought she was the loveliest woman I had ever seen. She was talking to some fellow, and when she laughed at a joke of his I decided he must be a humbug and went over to rescue her. It turned out she was from Boston like me; our parents lived only four miles apart and our families had friends in common. I was marveling at my luck when a little girl with red hair and freckles came skidding over and grabbed her arm, and I knew instantly that this was her daughter.

"This is Selene," said Christine proudly.

"Oh yea, hi," said Selene without glancing at me, already heading off again.

There was an awkward silence.

"Your daughter?" I asked vaguely. Christine seemed awfully young to have a daughter that age.

"Yes, isn't she beautiful?"

"Oh, yes. Definitely."

The conversation drifted.

"Are you married?" I finally asked.

"Oh, no," she said. "Never."

A reading began. A woman in tight jogging shorts began reciting poetry about limbs, digits, and orifices. The audience fell into rapt silence. I excused myself and retired outside with a fresh drink, breathing the April night. The stars flickered in the cold sky and a new moon rose over the elms, like a bright fingernail clipped from a goddess. An unmarried woman with a daughter? I was sensible enough to avoid that.

Soon Christine appeared in the doorway with the same humbug. Why was he following her around? I went over.

"You like the poetry?" I asked, striving for neutrality in tone. One had to be careful in a small town like Durango, Colorado; the poet was well known locally.

She made a face. All her freckles jammed together and her blue eyes crossed and her tongue stuck out and a sound, uncannily like retching, came from her throat. I had to laugh; it was so eloquent. I couldn't stop myself. "So, do you want to go horseback riding with me sometime?"

Two days later, Christine arrived for her ride. It was a warm April afternoon. I lived alone in the hills behind Durango, with two horses and a yellow dog. The snow was gone, and the pinyon woods behind my house were speckled with wild geraniums and senecio. The dead horse at the cattle pond had disappeared over the winter; the bones dragged off into the woods by the coyotes. Behind the ridge, another spring building boom had begun again, and in the mornings I could hear the grinding of bulldozers opening the earth.

Christine was wearing high-top red sneakers. Her short brown hair stuck out from under a baseball cap and the Colorado sun had browned the freckles on her nose and cheeks.

I was wearing a brand-new black cowboy hat and I thought it looked particularly authentic. I wanted to show her how well this

Boston Yankee-turned-cowboy could ride. I brought her down to the corral, and she watched while I worked on the horses. I brushed out their coats, picked their hooves, and saddled them up, murmuring soothing words, hoping they would behave.

I finished with Wilber the Appaloosa and went to bridle Redbone. Redbone was my favorite horse, of no recognizable breed, a perfect mutt, but nevertheless intelligent, full of heart, and possessed of an exquisite sense of mischief. Sensing the importance of the occasion, he clamped his jaws together and would not take the bit, shaking his head and throwing it back when I tried to slip it into his mouth.

This does not look good, I thought, while grabbing his ear and trying to pull his head down, my black hat being knocked off in the process.

"Do you need any help?" Christine asked.

"Oh no," I said. "This'll only take a second."

This had been a recurring problem with Redbone and he knew better, so I did what any respectable cowboy would do: I uttered a terrible oath and vigorously applied the side of my boot to his ribs. After that he couldn't open his mouth fast enough, but when I looked over at Christine, I saw the face of someone horrified to be having a first date with a horse-beater.

"This horse is a troublemaker," I said feebly. "He needs a firm hand."

"Oh," said Christine, backing away slightly.

"He knows perfectly well what he's supposed to do. He's just trying to make a fool out of me," I said.

"Of course," said Christine.

We rode across the pinyon hills behind the house and down into a deep valley called the Arroyo de los Chamisos. The arroyo has since been cut up with roads and developed, but back then it was still unspoiled, a bed of sand wandering between grassy embankments and tall ponderosas. The last of the snow was melting in the hills and a trickle of water threaded down the bottom. Under the warm sun the pines released a resinous scent.

We rode down the arroyo, splashing through the water, and skirted the old tank. A leg bone and hoof, with a rusted shoe attached, lay in the cheat grass. The horses could still smell death in the air and passed with a wary eye.

A mile down the wash, in a hidden meadow, we stopped. While the horses cropped the new grass, we sat under a big pine and talked about trivial things. With the nervousness of a teenager I finally kissed Christine. My mind was elsewhere when it came time to remount our horses, and Redbone (always mindful of an opportunity) spun sideways just as I swung into the saddle. I went right over the top and fell to the ground on the other side. Then the brute promptly stepped on my hand, and it swelled up like a cantaloupe. I tried to hide it but Christine noticed and made a terrible fuss.

"Oh no," she cried. "Every bone in your hand must be broken! You've got to see a doctor!"

I was mortified.

Despite the inauspicious beginning, we began seeing each other. Once, early on, I asked about Selene's father, and Christine replied that Selene was the product of immaculate conception. When I pressed the subject she replied, tartly, "He's in prison." It wasn't until later that I managed to drag the full story from her.

Christine spent her junior year of college in Paris, at the Sorbonne, and met him on a trip to Dublin. He was charming and sincere, as only an Irishman can be. He was a revolutionary and he talked, in soaring phrases, about freedom for Ireland and the equality of women. Christine was captivated. He followed her back to France and then to Boston.

There shortly followed the technical failure of a birth control device. They decided to make a go of it.

The trouble began around this time. He tried to force her to drop out of college. He complained that marriage was a bourgeois institution that enslaved women. He began to drink. She graduated college five months pregnant, with a degree in French literature.

He pressured her to go on welfare and Medicaid so he wouldn't have to pay for the birth, and made her apply for food stamps so he wouldn't have to buy food. His financial matters, he said, were none of her business. He spent all day in the cigarette and variety shop that he owned, selling stolen merchandise, and stayed out much of the night in the Boston bars, drinking and weeping about freedom for Ireland.

Selene rarely saw her father. For her first few birthdays, Christine had no money to buy presents, so she took home some toys from his shop, but he brought them back a week later and sold them. "She won't notice they're missing," he said. He was violent and abusive. He used to come home at night so drunk he would brush his teeth with the baby's Desitin.

One evening, Christine was watching the evening news. Suddenly there he was, with a dazed expression on his face, being shoved into a paddy wagon by men in brown suits. The FBI had videotaped him buying a planeload of automatic weapons, grenade launchers, and a redeye missile, destined for Northern Ireland.

It was the last she ever saw of him outside a prison cell.

The FBI had seized $10,000 he had secretly saved while Christine and Selene were on welfare and food stamps. The trial was quick and he was convicted and sentenced to nine years in prison, to be followed by deportation to his native country. Christine, for her daughter's sake, tried to stay in touch with him, sending him letters about Selene's progress, but he was angry at her and returned them unopened. At the same time, he wrote letters to Selene, chastising her for not writing him herself, as he was apparently unaware of the fact that a normal four- or five-year-old girl cannot read or write. The letters soon slowed to a trickle as he lost interest in his daughter, and those that did come had a hectoring, self-justifying tone and were full of strange pronouncements and dark allusions. They upset Selene terribly. Christine began to realize that he was not only abusive but potentially dangerous. She secretly left Boston, being careful to cover her tracks, and moved to Durango.

And where was he now?

He was about to be released from prison and deported. Christine had learned that he was looking for them. He wanted to take Selene away to Ireland. Christine heard, indirectly, from one of his brothers, that he had been threatening to have Selene kidnapped and taken out of the country, beyond the reach of American law.

And that, Christine explained to me, was how things stood.

I had heard all this late one night, in the living room of her house. The only light came from a fire, dying on the grate. When she finished, silence filled the room. The city was peaceful, and the fragrant small of pinyon hung in the air. There was the distant sound of a barking dog. Selene was sleeping quietly in the back bedroom, hugging a large stuffed tiger. Everything, in the fact of this story, suddenly seemed unreal, as if the evil of the world were seeping into the very air we were breathing.

Christine laughed nervously at the silence. "Aren't I just a terrible embarrassment? Aren't I difficult?" Then she added, shakily, "So what do you think?"

I didn't tell her what I thought. My thoughts were terrible. This was not at all a picture of the strong, independent woman that I had gotten to know. My life in the house on the hill, with two horses and a yellow dog, was orderly and calm. I had no enemies to speak of. I had always been careful to avoid unpleasant entanglements and hysterical love affairs.

I had many reasons for avoiding a commitment: my income from writing was too unstable, my house was too small, I hadn't met the right person. Most important, I felt that marriage was a dangerous business. Many of my friends who had married in their

twenties were already going through divorces of extreme vicious-
ness. Their children would be scarred for life and they financially
ruined. I reflected that these people had started fresh with all the
advantages: good careers, money, friends, supportive families.
They had not started with an IRA terrorist-kidnapper lurking in
the background. My life, in short, was exactly the way I wanted
it. I couldn't possibly take on a relationship with Christine. What
would happen, I thought, if I fell in love with this woman?

I broke it off as soon as I could. I didn't tell her why; in a parking lot behind the bank one sunny winter morning I said I was
sorry, that it wasn't working out, good-bye, and got in my car and
left, while she stood in the cold sun, crying and hurling insults
and pieces of ice.

Within twenty-four hours I had the greatest shock of my life:
I discovered that I was already in love with her. It was something I
had never felt before, so overwhelming that I could not even function without her. I also realized, to my utter consternation, that I
loved her daughter as if she were my own child.

Selene looked like an eight-year-old version of her mother,
glorious red hair, an archipelago of freckles across her face, eyes
the blue color of faraway hills, a dimple on her left cheek.

I loved Selene because, despite everything, she was so utterly
happy. She couldn't help it; she was one of those children who
loved being alive. Her life was not easy. They were very poor. They
had to turn off the heat in wintertime, switching it back on only
to keep the pipes from freezing. Christine worked seventy hours
a week as a baker, getting up at five o'clock every morning. Selene
was lonely and missed Boston. And yet, every night she sang herself to sleep, and I could always tell when she awoke by the joyful
song bursting from her room. Gershwin, Cole Porter, Louis Arm-
strong, Rodgers and Hammerstein, she knew them all. She did
cartwheels and handstands and squealed with delight when I ran
around her with her clinging to my back like a monkey.

When Selene and Christine moved in, I built a tiny room for her by walling off part of our bedroom. In the mornings, Selene would crawl out of bed in the dark and get into our bed, and squirm and burrow and giggle until she had firmly wedged herself between me and Christine. If I touched Christine or kissed her good morning Selene would cry out, "Hey! No touching!"

Every night when I came in to say goodnight she demanded a story. Her favorites were the stories of bad things I had done as a child. "Tell me about the time you put the dead skunk on the Ginns' doorstep and set it on fire!" she would cry out, or: "Tell me about when you shot a bottle rocket at the police car!" Whenever I tried to leave she clung to me like an octopus, wheedling and begging another story, demanding hugs and kisses at the same time. I found her irresistible.

She was a brilliant and unusual child. She thought television was boring. Instead she read books, devouring them at the rate of ten to twenty a week. She was intensely curious about the world but tried to feign indifference.

"So Selene," I said, "do you know what's beyond the edge of the universe?"

"No, and I don't care."

And then a day later she said, "There is no edge to the universe, so there, Mr. Know-it-all."

At eight she could calculate whole-number square roots, cube roots, and fourth roots in her head. If she got bored with the dinner table conversation, she sometimes demanded: "Give me a problem!"

"What is the cube root of 216?" I asked.

She crawled under the dining room table. We could hear her giggling for five minutes.

"Six?" her muffled voice came up tentatively from underneath.

When we got up we found that, in addition to figuring out the problem, she had tied all our shoelaces to the chair legs.

There was, however, an undercurrent of tension in my relationship with Selene. Ours was not a simple relationship; it had an unfortunate complexity. For the truth was, Selene was not sure if she even liked me. As far back as she could remember she had had her mother to herself. My intrusion into this satisfactory state of affairs was unwelcome.

Even at eight Selene knew her feelings were irrational and she tried to control them, but they erupted often. She was sometimes sullen and rude, and made a point of principle to refuse to do anything I asked.

Once I made the mistake of pressing her a little too hard. She finally erupted, "You're not my dad and you have no right to make me do anything!"

In October, under a fat cottonwood in the playground of Selene's school, Christine asked me to marry her. I hemmed and hawed and we had a rather heated discussion. When she pressed me I brought up the fact that I had to think about it since I would, after all, be taking on a threat from a convicted IRA terrorist-gunrunner who was at that very moment plotting to kidnap her daughter.

She accused me of cowardice. "If you really loved us," she said, "you would take on any danger for me and Selene. You would want to protect us instead of running away."

She finally told me that I'd better hurry up and decide, because if I thought she was going to wait, then I was a bigger fool than I looked. I'd never find another woman like her nor could I expect to have a daughter as wonderfully brought up as Selene, or as lively and pretty and intelligent, and therefore the decision should be obvious to anyone with common sense. Under the rustling yellow light of the cottonwood and the autumnal aroma of pinyon smoke, she said, "If you miss this opportunity, you'll regret it for the rest of your life."

I eventually had to agree. I knew from the outset that I didn't have a choice, and that I loved her and Selene (despite the fact that Selene didn't love me). We set the wedding date for July.

Selene tried to be happy about the impending marriage, but she was moody. She was particularly upset when she learned we were thinking of going on a honeymoon without her. "You can't wait to get rid of me," she cried.

One day that winter we found ourselves on a long drive to Salt Lake City.

As usual, Selene called for a story. "Tell me about the time you blew up the golf course," she squealed.

Christine turned to her. "You know, Selene, soon Doug and I are going to be married."

"Yeah, I know," she said.

"Maybe you might start thinking about calling him something other than 'Doug.'"

There was a sudden, unbearable silence.

"Like what," Selene said flatly.

"He is going to be your dad, you know," Christine said.

There was another long silence. The wheels hummed on the road. I felt my face burning. I liked Christine's directness, but this was going a little too far.

"No," Selene said.

"What do you mean, 'no'?" Christine asked. "Why not?"

"Because I don't want to," she said firmly.

"It's O.K.," I said hastily. "Selene can call me whatever she wants."

"Will you think about it?" Christine asked, looking intently at her daughter.

Selene was silent, staring out the window at the barren Utah desert, covered with windblown snow. I felt my heart sink; I felt unaccountably hurt, although she'd been calling me "Doug" now for over a year and I knew perfectly well she wasn't going to change.

Later I asked Christine never to bring up the subject with Selene again.

"I just wanted to put the idea in her head," she said. "Now it's up to you."

"Up to me what?"

"To win her over."

Douglas Preston is the author of five books, including the acclaimed *Cities of Gold,* the best-selling novel *Jennie,* the thriller *Relic,* and the nonfiction title, *Talking to the Ground: One Family's Journey on Horseback Across the Sacred Land of the Navajo,* from which this story was excerpted.

Jimbo

Rick Bass

Everyone loves to be a teacher. Of course, it's easy to see why this love has survived over the generations: it favors the species, certainly. The magic in learning is no stronger than the pleasure of teaching something: giving a part of yourself, and having someone take it.

There was a bully when I was small who used to beat me up regularly. If I rode my bike through his neighborhood, he would chase me down on foot, push me off the bike, and let me have it. Once by massive misfortune we were on the same baseball team. And there was some rule whereby everyone had to pitch. This athletic bully's team, our team, was winning about 3,000 to nothing until it got to be my inning to pitch.

They started catching up real fast.

The bully, whose name was Jimbo, shouted at me from third base. Several times he started toward the mound, ignoring the other team's runners, who kept circling the bases faster and faster. Jimbo banged his fist in his glove and told me all the things that were going to happen to me.

You could see the desperation on his face when this did nothing to improve my pitching. It was like the worst dreams: I wasn't getting the ball near the plate, even after his threats. I aimed at the plate, praying that when the batters wapped the ball someone would make a miraculous catch, but my pitches starting going behind their backs, over the catcher's head, everywhere. It was as if I had a sudden serious physical disability. The ball was going about halfway between the plate and the dugout, at a 45-degree angle away from where it was supposed to be.

Jimbo stormed over and grabbed the ball and put it in my fist. He showed me a way to grip it that I'd never seen done. Then he took it back from me and with his tremendously hateful, determined scowl, showed me, without actually releasing the ball, how to throw it. He demonstrated in a slow, barely contained, angry motion, the reaching, pulling, aiming.

"Pretend with your free hand like you're pushing someone out of the way," he said. It was easy to see that that was what he was thinking of. His hand concealed the ball until the last moment; then, shoving (slowly, for my benefit) the imaginary, offensive person aside—there was a sudden opening where that person and his free, gloved hand were—like spit and hate, Jimbo threw the ball through there, through that clawed gap of air, a strike and made the catcher yell "Ouch!"

I tried it and threw strikes. He stood there on the mound and watched to make sure I did it right. I was relieved and amazed. I remember his face: he grinned and hid his own amazement. I don't think he had ever taught anyone anything before. I don't think anyone had ever listened.

I threw more strikes. We won the game. The next day Jimbo beat me up. But I knew there was something else in him no one understood: I think I was the first person ever to see it, and was amazed that even an ogre who drubbed me could feel that sensation. The last I heard of him, he was in jail. He couldn't, or wouldn't, spell or write, and in my most tearful moments, tasting my own blood, I would remind him of this. But he could teach you how to throw a baseball better, I suspect, than it has ever been done. There is a tremendous amount of genius in being able to take someone throwing wildly into the dugout and tell him one sentence and have the ball go precisely over the plate.

If I was angry enough, or desperate enough, could I tell someone how to find oil so well that he or she could go out and do it immediately? Could I do it in one sentence? Not even in my most confident moments do I imagine that I could. I do not know what that sentence is. I think that Jimbo was a genius, and hope he got out of jail. The closest I can come to that sentence, beyond "Listen to the earth," is that you have to get down under and beyond the more occupational greed and look into the simplicity, the purity, the secret part of it—the act, not the results, and yourself—and be aware that it is history, buried.

Jimbo's sentences were so much shorter. He would scowl at what I just said and beat me up.

A petroleum geologist and environmental activist, Rick Bass is the author of five works of nonfiction about the outdoors and the prize-winning story collections *The Watch, Platte River,* and *In the Loyal Mountains.*

Eyes on Another World

CONNIE MCDOUGALL

When my twelve-year-old son and I saw the movie *Apollo 13*, I told him a true story, about how his apparently ordinary mother once had a personal acquaintance with the last man on the moon.

Back in the early 1980s, I was a radio news reporter in Albuquerque, and the astronaut, having left NASA, was a U.S. Senator from New Mexico. This situation put me in frequent contact with him, which usually involved sticking a microphone in his face and asking questions.

All through his answers, I kept thinking: *My gosh, just look at him. He walked on the moon. He was the last one there. He saw impossibly rare and startling things, but now here he is, spilling words into my hand.*

One day I covered a presidential visit. This didn't happen very often in Albuquerque, and never to me. We local media types were corralled onto a bandstand about five feet above the airport's tarmac while national press and VIPs roamed free at ground level. That's where the senator was: The last man on the moon was schmoozing. After all, the president had come to bolster GOP reelection campaigns, including, as I recall, the senator's.

"Hello, Senator Schmitt," I called down to him from my perch. "It's a big day, I guess."

"It certainly is," he smiled, happy as can be.

Harrison "Jack" Schmitt was the first scientist to become an astronaut. A geologist, he was part of the three-man *Apollo 17* mission in December 1972—the last moon landing. He hip-hopped across gray powder at a place called Taurus-Littrow, scooping, digging, and hauling back more than 240 pounds of moon.

Ten years later, he worked crowds, not rocks, glad-handing for votes on a hot, dusty runway. I thought I could still see the missileman in him, though. He was like his spaceship: compact and tightly wired. His lapels lay flat across a tidy chest, and despite the rising heat, he stood cracker dry.

Jack was a handsome man, dark with especially nice teeth. His eyes combined intensity and distance, taking you in then moving on. Under their gaze, you could feel uplifted and suddenly drab, like common stone.

He paced the asphalt waiting for the president, then pointed to the sky. "There it is," he said, and *Air Force One* appeared out of the flat, blue sky.

It landed, taxied, and pulled to a stop parallel to us. I was about to broadcast live, but the plane was too far away for me to pick President Reagan out of the crowd.

"Senator," I called out. "I can't see from here. When he comes out, let me know will you?" He smiled and nodded up to me. He could see fine.

In my headphones I heard the anchor toss it to me: "And for that report we go live to the Albuquerque International Airport..."

My cue. I was on the air with no president in sight. "*Air Force One* has indeed landed, touching down just moments ago to enthusiastic applause. President Reagan has not yet emerged, although we expect his presence any time now..."

I stalled. I talked about *Air Force One*, about the dignitaries, including the senator who glanced up at me and shook his head—no president yet. I talked about the national press, now at their swarming peak.

At last, the senator spotted Reagan and tried to signal me. But I was occupied on the air, squinting at the plane. He stretched up to the only thing within his reach and gave my ankle a gentle shake. In deep and important tones, I proceeded to announce: "Senator Schmitt has just grabbed my ankle to say President Reagan is here."

What? Horrified, I shot a look at him, but he didn't seem to notice. He grinned and set off to meet the president.

I couldn't stop the report to explain my circumstances, so I plunged on. The president arrives, the president waves, the president shakes the senator's hand. They wave, they leave.

When it was over, I raced back to the station. Maybe no one noticed. I walked in, and the anchor jumped up, "He grabbed what?!"

Humiliating as it was, the moment held a secret thrill for me. A hand that had once sifted moon dust and ancient rubble had circled my ankle. In this small way, I touched the moon.

Months later, Jack gave a presentation to an elementary school in Albuquerque's South Valley, a poor area. I was sent over to do a feature. As I pulled up in my news car, I saw him on the sidewalk collecting his things—stunning slides of moonscapes. He walked in alone, no entourage. By that time he'd lost the election, so he was both a former astronaut and a former senator. Carrying a briefcase in one hand, a box in the other, he might have been selling brushes.

I sat in the bleachers with the youngsters while he operated the projector, explaining each photo in his brisk and hearty manner. The man in the business suit talked about the man in the spacesuit. "There I am," he said, "on the moon."

There he was, all right, next to the American flag with Earth above his shoulder like a pretty blue parrot. One knee of his spacesuit was sooty from kneeling in the dust.

When the show ended, he took questions, and then gave the kids a little pep talk about staying in school. They applauded and filed out.

Only twelve men walked on the moon, and the last among them stood in the middle of a basketball court packing up slides.

Out on the sidewalk we chatted. The cicadas were building to their afternoon din.

"Jack," I said, turning to look him in the eye. He was perhaps two feet away from me and I could see the lines in his face. "Are you in a rush?" He wasn't. "Then will you..." I closed my eyes and opened them again. "Could you tell me what it was like?"

And so he did. I think he wanted to tell me. Sharing his experience was part of the mission, and he gave it to anyone who would listen: presidents, little kids, awestruck reporters.

He sat on the passenger side of my car in a South Valley parking lot and gave me his story. The astronaut gestured with his hands and looked out the window at a stand of cottonwood trees. He raised his eyes to the sky and because I couldn't see that far, he told me what was out there.

He seemed to talk for quite a long time. I said very little because I wanted him to go on and on. I wanted the sun to set and the moon to rise so he could point to the place.

But the time came when he had to leave. I watched him go and as I remember it, he left a trail of gray powder prints behind.

This is the story I tell my son. I don't think he understands why these events are important to me. It's just that when Jack described his journey, I got to go, too. We paused in the dust; we looked up and saw the Earth waiting like a mother in a doorway for him to come home.

Freelancer Connie McDougall writes newspaper and magazine articles on various topics including travel and culture. Now that the kids are grown, she's also writing poetry and is currently working on her first novel.

In My Father's Footsteps

DINA KLUGMAN CRAMER

My father was not a religious man. He had been raised a good practicing Jew in Europe; they didn't have many reform or modern Jews there; if you were Jewish you generally went in for the whole thing. But the Holocaust changed everything, and after it was over he had no more relationship with the deity or any other aspect of religious practice. What good had any of it been? My father had always been a giver and one who had a profound sense of responsibility to his community, both locally and worldwide. And so, still young, he willed his body to a medical school upon his death, wanting to find one last way to serve his fellow man. Thus when he died four years ago at age seventy-seven, his body was whisked off to the medical school, and there was no marker of any kind for his family. We all approved of and supported his decision, but it did leave us a little empty. However, there is one place on this earth where there is a marker and testimonial to his life. It is a plaque in a tiny French village in the mountainous pre-Alps. How that plaque got there is a whole story. Last summer, I visited the village both to see the plaque and to meet the villagers who thought as highly of him as he did of them.

The village is named Prelenfrey-du-Gua. It is a dozen winding uphill miles from Grenoble, in the Vercors Mountains. Although today it takes only thirty or forty minutes by car from Grenoble, during the thirties and forties, when not everyone had a car, and it was served by a little bus, it seemed worlds away from Grenoble, and in fact, from anywhere. My father called it the village at the end of the world. As it turned out, escaping Grenoble and arriving at the village meant the difference between life and death to many Jews during the German occupation of World War II. But this was a secret which was not uncovered until forty years after the war was over, and it was my father who uncovered it. Through his research he revealed the life-risking courage of the villagers who had hidden Jews in their homes during the war. As a result, the village was awarded the Medal of the Righteous from Yad Vashem, the holocaust museum in Jerusalem, and the village's leading family who masterminded the plot to save the Jews was given individual medals and had their names inscribed in the wall of the holocaust museum in Jerusalem and the holocaust museum in Washington.

How did my father happen to come upon this story? Well, it goes back to the 1930s when he and his mother settled in Grenoble, having emigrated from Germany to get away from Hitler, little knowing that he would follow them. My father's mother was fearful that he might contract tuberculosis because his father had died of it, and it was a rather common scourge in those days. Luckily they lived at the foot of the pre-Alps where there were sanatoriums and preventoriums, places where people went to "take the air" and strengthen their lungs. A "preventorium" was an observation sanatorium, intended to "prevent" serious illness. The doctor they consulted recommended that my father, then thirteen, spend the summer at a friendly, family-run preventorium in Prelenfrey, a kind of summer camp with lots of other kids, where he could run around in the fresh mountain air. He returned on school vacations over the next six years, and had wonderful memories of those summers, and the friendliness of the large, extended family that ran the village and the preventorium (which they called the "Prevent"), which was the village's main industry. He says they were a clan, all working together. If, when you arrived, there was no room for you in the preventorium itself, not to worry, there was always a spare bed in the home of Oncle Auguste, or some other family member.

It was this tradition of hospitality that led them to take in and shelter the desperate Jews who were to show up on their door-steps only a few years later. By then, my father was gone, having escaped from France clandestinely, and having joined the Free French Army under General de Gaulle. Because he was away fighting during the entire war, he knew nothing about what was going on in Prelenfrey. Nor did he give the village any thought afterward. After the war, everything was different. His mother had been taken away and murdered at Auschwitz; he had married my mother in Palestine during the war; he had to start making a living and supporting a family. And in 1948, facing food and housing shortages in France, my parents, with thirteen-month-old me, made a grand move to California, an adopted homeland that treated them well and where they adjusted happily. We were a bilingual, bicultural family, but we were Americans foremost and became naturalized American citizens at the first opportunity.

Skip ahead thirty-four years, to 1982. My father, now retired, decided that on a trip to France it would be interesting to go back to the village of his teenage summers and see how it was today. He and my mother made the trip. The first time they tried to take the little winding road from Grenoble, it was so foggy that they had to turn back. They tried again the next day and arrived at the village. The son of the village leaders of that time, Georges Guidi, known as Jo and today eighty years old, recounted to me what happened when my parents arrived. He was upstairs and had just woken from his nap. The housekeeper answered the knock at the door. He heard through the open window someone ask after each member of the family. To each query, the housekeeper answered, "*mort*," dead. Finally my father came to Jo Guidi. "Ah, he is upstairs having his *sieste*." At this point Jo said to himself: "This is someone who knows the whole family. I must go see who it is." He came to the front door, and my father said to him (in French of course), "Guess who I am?" Jo answered, "You must be David Klugman." There was no doubt, he said; no one else had such erect posture and bearing.

During the course of an afternoon's visit with Jo, my father asked him what had happened in the village during the war and occupation. And so the story of the village's role in hiding and protecting the Jews came out. My father was fairly well amazed, and filed the story in the back of his mind. He was working on other projects at the time and gave it no more thought then. But he said the story must have been working in his subconscious, because a full ten years later it hit him what an important story it was, and that it needed to be told, and it looked like he was the person to tell it.

That story was that Jo's parents, Andre and Helene Guidi, used the preventorium to hide Jewish children and gave them false identities. They also found homes for adults and some of the older children in the surrounding farms. Altogether they were responsible for saving fifty-one Jews, twenty of them children. I calculate that this comes to one Jew saved for every four villagers. The elder Guidis orchestrated this conspiracy of silence.

The village may have been "at the end of the world," but the Germans found it. By pre-arrangement with the postmistress in Grenoble, on the day the Germans were to invade Prelenfrey she gave a very brief signal, which was all she could do, but it was enough. By plan the children were sent higher in the mountains to hide in a shepherd's hut. They were told not to come down until they saw sheets hanging on the line in the village. They had performed this drill numerous times when they received false alarms, but this was the real thing. Daniel Szydlo, today a retired doctor in Paris, was one of the leaders of the children. He and many of the others involved gave my father notarized testimony of the events from which my father wrote a book about the events, *The Conspiracy of the Righteous.*

On July 22, 1944, 300 Germans marched into the village (whose population was only 200) and announced that by 10:00 A.M. they wanted all the men between the ages of sixteen and sixty lined up against the school wall, which was along the main road. Jo showed me the wall that was directly opposite his house. It was well known that this part of the mountains was a center of resistance. At the appointed time thirty-two men lined up, while the Germans shouldered their machine guns to shoot them. Suddenly a nineteen-year-old nurse from the preventorium came out and shouted at them to stop. These were not resisters she said; they were simple peasants who knew nothing. Besides she needed some strong men to push a wheelbarrow of supplies up the hill to the preventorium. Astonished, the soldiers lowered their guns, and after consulting among themselves, decided to take all the men to Gestapo headquarters in Grenoble for questioning. Jo told me that once there he was selected at random to lower his pants and show whether he was circumcised, which he was not. "I had a Jew in front of me and a Jew behind me, he says, and by some stroke of luck, they chose me. I had a beard, so maybe they thought I looked Jewish." The men were all questioned and asked to tell where the Jews were. Not one single one broke down; not a one said they knew anything about any Jews. The men were kept in jail for four days, and then all told to "get out of here."

With the exception of Jo's mother and one other family, who were Protestant, the rest of the village was Catholic, some practicing, some not. None of the villagers had ever met any Jews before or had much idea what a Jew was. But they had an innate sense of what was right. They didn't like oppression whether it was against Jews or anyone else. My father always felt that the story wasn't about Jews; it was about justice and what was right. He long wondered why the village had acted as they had. He concluded that they had a sense of moral right and wrong and a dislike for authority, as well as a hospitable tradition.

Interestingly, once the war was over, and the Jews had gone, no one ever talked about these events, not even among themselves. Most of the Jews had no further contact with the village. The nurse, Anne O., never even told her own children about the events or her part in them. It was not until my father began his research and tracked down the participants all over the world, that they began to speak in effusive terms of the courage shown by the Guidi family and the rest of the village.

My father worked hard to bring the village's story to the attention of the authorities in Israel, and as a result the medal was given to the village in a big ceremony held fifty years to the day from the events at the school wall, on July 22, 1994. As part of the program of the day, a conference was held in which witness after witness testified about the events of fifty years before, breaking a fifty-year silence at last. Afterward a huge party was held, attended by a representative of the Israeli Embassy and many French dignitaries; bands played, flags waved. Prelenfrey finally received the recognition it deserved.

The preventorium had been closed in the sixties due to advances in the field of medicine. Doctors began treating tuberculosis with drugs, Jo told me. Today, the building is sadly run down. My father had wanted the village to consider reopening it as a conference center, hotel, or school but nothing came of the idea. He cared very much about the village, and they knew it. He maintained his relationship with the village and the individuals in it and continued to visit occasionally until his death. When he died, the villagers wanted to commemorate him in some way, so they hit upon the idea of the plaque. The plaque lists his military medals, as well as his work for Prelenfrey and mentions that he was once a patient of the preventorium (*"ancien du Prevent"*). They put it right next to the plaque they had received for their courage during the Holocaust.

I think a word about Jo Guidi will illustrate the independent spirit of these mountain people. Jo is a free-thinking, iconoclastic old man. An atheist and leftist, who believes that the least government is the best government, he refuses to set foot in the village church which is right next to his house. His sense of rightness says that a nonbeliever should not step on a site which is holy to another. However, in a funny twist, when the cross on a pedestal which sits in the center of town was knocked over by a speeding motorist, he and his non-believing Protestant friend fought for years to have the government replace it. "We, the atheists, fought the hardest for that cross," he said, "because it was part of the patrimony of the village." Now this clearly is someone who thinks for himself.

It seems that some things never change. When I first arrived in Grenoble by train from Paris and got in the taxi line, the taxi ahead of me refused the party in front of me and took me instead. Curious, I asked him why he had refused the other party. "Oh," he answered, "they were going to a place in the mountains that treats the lungs, and I didn't have time to take them there. I have an appointment, but I have time to take you because your hotel is not far." He couldn't have known how amazed I was by his response—I had just arrived, and my father's story was already coming to life.

And Prelenfrey continues its tradition of hospitality. When I visited, Jo sent one of his friends to pick me up at my Grenoble hotel, and I spent the whole day with a group of them, talking (I was grateful I had been made to learn French as a child), touring the area, and of course eating the fine food prepared for the occasion. It was an extraordinary opportunity to get in touch with both the early and the late parts of my father's life, and helped me put him to rest.

Dina Klugman Cramer was born in France in 1947 and has lived in the United States since 1948. She was raised near San Francisco and now lives in the Los Angeles area where she is Head of the Reference Department at the El Segundo Public Library. She loves everything French and thinks that Franco-American tension is silly and mostly a media creation.

The 007 Rule

MICHAEL CRICHTON

The crew stretches a white bed sheet in the middle of a field so the helicopter will know where to land. A crowd of local people line the fences around the field. They stare at the sheet, waiting for something to happen. Their attention turns the sheet into a work of art, a Christo. *Wrapped Irish Farm Field, 1978*. I would find it funny if we weren't behind schedule.

It is eight in the morning and bitterly cold. We are in a provincial train station outside Mullingar, Ireland, about to start a week of filming on top of a speeding train. Sean Connery has agreed to do his own stunts on top of the train. The little 1863 locomotive is hissing steam in front of the station, with our specially constructed coaches trailing behind. It's time to start filming, but the camera helicopter has not arrived yet from England. I suggest a test ride on the train. We climb up a ladder onto the roof of the cars, and set off.

Within minutes Connery is grinning like a kid on a carnival ride. He's a superb athlete who could have been a professional footballer. Now he hops lightly from car to car, thoroughly enjoying himself. We approach a bridge, and must lie flat on the deck. The bridge whips over us, inches from our faces. Connery laughs uproariously, "Bloody fantastic!"

We return to the station and begin shooting. The exhilaration fades, and the work becomes work. Constant vigilance is required. The Irish Railways have permitted us to use twenty miles of track in the most beautiful part of the country, but since this is Ireland, the twenty bridges that span the rails are all of different heights. Some are very low. We have previously mapped and measured each bridge, but no one is willing to trust a map. Before each shot, we creep slowly beneath the bridge, to check our clearance.

Even more dangerous are the telephone and electrical wires that sometimes span the track; these are unmarked and difficult to see until the last moment.

Then, too, our authentic period locomotive spews a stream of flowing cinders and ash back at us. We literally set the countryside on fire wherever we go. Each night, when we return home, I take a shower and wash my hair. The water hits the tub inky black.

Connery throws himself into his work with abandon. He is one of the most remarkable people I have ever met, lighthearted and serious at the same moment. I have learned a great deal from being around him. He is at ease with himself, and is direct and frank. "I like to eat with my fingers," he says, eating with his fingers in a fancy restaurant, not giving a damn. You cannot embarrass him with trivialities. Eating is what's important. People come over for an autograph and he glowers at them "I'm *eating*," he says sternly. "Come back later." They come back later, and he politely signs their menus. He doesn't hold grudges unless he intends to. "I spent a lot of my life being miserable," he says. "Then one day I thought, I'm here for the day, I can enjoy the day or not. I decided I might as well enjoy it." There is that quality about him, that sense of choice and control over himself and his moods. It makes him integrated, self-assured. The most common remark about him is, "That's a *real man*."

Once, on an airplane, a woman sighs, "Oh, you're so *masculine*." Connery laughs. "But I'm very feminine," he insists. And he means it; and he delights in that side of himself. A gifted mimic, he likes to rehearse alone, playing all the parts himself. He does startlingly accurate imitations of everyone in the cast, including Donald and Lesley-Anne, his leading lady. He always seems to enjoy himself. He takes pleasure in all his aspects, all his appetites.

I am not equally open, and he teases me. Once, after a shot, I feel his hand gestures were a little effeminate. I call for a retake, but I'm not sure how to tell Sean what needs to be changed. How do you tell 007 that he's effeminate?

"Sean, on that last shot, you had a hand gesture…"

"Yes, what about it? I thought it was good."

"Well, uh, it was a little, uh, loose. Limp."

His eyes narrow. "What are you trying to say?"

"Well, it could be a bit crisper. Stronger, you know."

"Stronger…"

"Yes. Stronger."

"You're saying I look like a poof?" Now he's grinning, amused at my discomfort.

"Yes. A little."

"Well, just say so, ducky!" he roars. "Just say what you want! We haven't got all day!" And he shoots the scene again, with a different gesture.

Later he takes me aside. "You know," he says, "you don't do any favors beating about the bush. Making us try and deduce what you mean. You think you're being polite, but you're actually just difficult. Say what you mean and get on with it."

I promise to try. And I do better, but I never manage to be as direct as he is. He says. "You should always tell the truth, because if you tell the truth you make it the other person's problem."

He follows his own dictum: he always tells the truth. Sean seems to live in a kind of present moment, responding to events with an unaffected immediacy that disregards people I know he doesn't like. Sometimes he blows up angrily at his close friends. He always tells the truth as he sees it at the moment, and if somebody doesn't like it, it's their problem.

Michael Crichton was born in Chicago. After graduating from Harvard Medical School, he embarked on a career as a writer and filmmaker. Called "the father of the techno-thriller," his novels include *The Andromeda Strain, Congo, Jurassic Park, Rising Sun. The Lost World, Timeline,* and *Prey,* a story about nanotechnology run amok. His latest novel is *State of Fear.* He has also written four nonfiction books, including *Five Patients, Jasper Johns,* and his autobiography, *Travels,* from which this piece was excerpted.

The Dump Run

MOLLY HILLIARD

Once again, I had made a major life decision. This time, I'd decided to quit my city job, get rid of my belongings, buy a camper van, and set off in new directions—alone. I had made crazy decisions like this before, like the time I moved to Scotland with a six-month work visa, or the time I quit my job at a prosperous investment firm to take web design classes. But after seven years of safety and stability in the city of San Francisco, this latest "new, fun idea" was daunting.

Quitting my job was actually the easy part. After sacrificing two years of breath and blood to a non-profit organization, my boss gave me my first official review. Fully confident I would get rave reviews as usual (not to claim bragging rights, but I am a hard worker), I was devastated when she tore me apart. Having the confidence and experience to know that these were her issues and not mine, with a little shakiness in my voice and a big smile on my face, I told her I was moving on.

Buying the camper van, a 1986 Westfalia Volkswagen Vanagon, was a bigger challenge. Although I have owned five cars, my dear old daddy had always bought and sold them for me. Now, I summoned my courage from great visions: leaving San Francisco after so many years of hard work, challenging myself in the ways of independence, seeing the country and living out of my van for as long as I chose. These were my motivators.

With a huge gulp and a giant leap of faith, I wrote a check for $8,800 to Sam, the twenty-four-year-old surfer/Westfalia mechanic, who told me he would rather die by being eaten by a shark than any other way. I figured that had to mean something, and into my life came AlmaShark (a homage to Sam, and my little Spanish Soul Cruiser). She can be testy and likes a lot of gas, but she is a roving house on wheels. What a beauty!

With these two huge tasks completed, all I had left to do was pack up, move out, and head down the road. Well, after one week of packing, garage sales, donating, and cleaning, I thought I would be on my way. But it somehow took another four days of packing, donating, and cleaning to get there. Two days before I finally left, I had to make a dump run.

Now, being a recycler to my very core, the mere thought of going to the dump with anything just killed me. But what else to do with your old, rickety shelves no one will buy, your chairs even the Salvation Army won't take, and your wicker things your friends don't want? They go to the dump. So, with instructions from my landlord, I drove down to the Pacific Transition Dump—a place to unload your garbage, where for a small fee, they smash it to bits before taking it to the real dump. I was relieved. At least I would not have to face a huge dump, seagulls circling above the smoggy stench of hundreds of acres of wasteland.

So off I went, AlmaShark loaded almost beyond capacity. At the very top of the pile were the soundboards and corrugated metal one of my roommates had nailed to the walls for a "Sci-Fi Look." I had learned during loading that this metal stuff hurts my office-soft hands, so I did what any normal City Gurl would do—I donned my biking gloves for protection.

Those of us lucky enough to have lived in the Bay Area know the route to Pacifica, the town just south of San Francisco on the ocean. Leaving San Francisco on Highway 280 south, you travel up the foggy hills until the ocean opens up in front of you. The wide expanse of blue, the Santa Cruz Mountains in the background, and the fog rolling out to sea, it is breathtaking. Then it hit me: why do I want to leave here? One of the most beautiful places on Earth, where countless cultures mix, and the land and sea, the mountains and redwoods sit in their majestic beauty? I took a deep breath, assured myself about my choices, and took the Manor Exit to the Transition Dump.

Following the shore, up the hills, sand dunes between me and the ocean, I pulled into the dump. Feeling as naïve as they come, I hopped out and waited for the Dump Guy to tell me what to do. He checked out my load, priced it at $20, and told me to back her into the corner. The smell was intense. The dump is an immense three-sided building, about one hundred feet high, with no floors. The guy next to me had a truck with a back lift to dump it all in. Next to him, a bulldozer was smashing remains into the wall.

I opened up AlmaShark from the back and side, put on my biking gloves and got to work. First the corrugated metal, then the soundboard, and then my bags of trash. The more I tossed, the more my energy rose. When I got to the unwanted chairs, I hurled them as hard and far as I could. This felt good! I thought it was my guilty pleasure of doing the unthinkable—throwing away things that could be fixed and used again. The grill from the departed upstairs neighbor, an old stool with origins unknown—I threw them as hard as I could.

Then I glanced at a lamp I had owned…forever. A beat-up wicker hanging lamp my dad had given me from his house when I started college. Damn—that thing was ugly! I had spray painted it blue over its original brown, and it was bent, torn, unsellable, and undonatable. Hell, I didn't even want it. So why did the sight of it bring sudden, stinging tears to my eyes?

That's when I realized that this feeling of bliss and excited energy wasn't from a guilty pleasure; it was from the feeling of freedom. The decision to change my life's course encompassed so much for me. I was now starting on a new path, living more simply and being as independent as I could muster. I needed to let go of all of these old things to start on my new path. And I was doing it, physically doing it! Out went the milk crates, the mattress, and those horrible porch chairs—stained and sun-bleached. I felt so liberated!

I was finished. I closed AlmaShark's back hatch, went around to her side, and then I saw it again—the old, battered, wicker lamp. I had forgotten that I had purposely saved that for last. The last piece, a relic from my childhood that had traveled with me for fifteen years. I grabbed it and let it swing. As it soared high above the heap of trash, I heard myself let out a yelp, and felt more tears stinging my eyes. I quickly jumped into Alma, made it past the line of trucks waiting their turn, and hit the road next to the dunes and along the ocean.

Then the tears fell, fell so very hard. I was free! I did it! I had given myself the space to make real changes and live in adventure. I was starting to let go of my known world and embrace the un-known. My chest was full, and the sky was so blue.

Then the giggles started.

Who knew such enlightenment could come from a dump run?

Since leaving her city life in San Francisco, Molly Hilliard has traveled to Central America, spent time back home in Indiana and now works in Northern Spain as a hiking guide on the Camino de Santiago. During the winter months she skis, works, and writes in the Rocky Mountains. You can reach her at mizmols@yahoo.com

Daju

ROBERT J. MATTHEWS

It was almost winter, and nearing the end of my stay in Kathmandu, much of my time was occupied with saying good-bye. I had gotten to know many new people on this particular visit, but those persons whom I most actively sought out were those whom I had gotten to know the least.

They were waiters, merchants, black-market money changers; they were little children and old women who sold matches and single cigarettes along damp, narrow streets. I certainly did not know these people as one knows a friend or even an acquaintance for that matter, but for the past several months they had been my landmarks along countless streets and in innumerable restaurants, and they were by now as familiar to me as any back home. It was this collection of little faces, brief greetings, and equally brief conversations that always endeared Nepal to me.

Upon finding one of these persons prior to my departure, I rarely would actually say good-bye. Instead, I found that all I really wanted to do was just look at them once more; to memorize them in their world, perhaps foolishly thinking that the moment could later be recalled with the same life and clarity as the original.

Sometimes, in my marginal Nepali, I would say that I am returning to my own country. Most often the reply was simply a smile, accompanied by the characteristic little sideways nod of the head which in Nepal means understanding. And that was all.

One person with whom I did speak was an old man I used to see almost every day. He seemed to spend most of his time just sitting in the sun on a small, raised wooden platform next to an outdoor marketplace where aggressive women with clumps of wrinkled and faded rupees in their fists deftly negotiated the cacophonous buying and selling of fruits and vegetables.

The first time I saw him he smiled at me. He said nothing, nor did I stop to speak with him. I recall giving him a rather cursory smile in return, and then continued on my way without another thought. A few days later I saw him again, still seated in the same place. As I passed him he smiled at me again just as he had before. I was taken by how sincere this man's expression was, and also how peaceful he seemed to be. I smiled back and offered the traditional *Namaste*, which he returned. I could not quite explain why, but it was that ingenuous smile of his that many times made me detour just to see him and say hello.

Eventually I found that he spoke a few words of English, and occasionally we would have a cigarette together and exchange pleasantries. Sometimes, after dinner, I would walk through the silent streets that were now only sporadically lit by the incidence of weak light insinuating itself through greasy restaurant windows. Then I would come upon him, still seated in the same place. He would be sitting quietly, smoking, and drinking tea out of the ubiquitous glass tumbler that someone had probably bought for him.

One evening, on my way back to my room after dinner, I saw him in his usual spot, and I stopped to say hello. For the first time since I had known him, I glimpsed his feet protruding from under the rough woolen blanket that always covered him.

They were severely misshapen and deeply ulcerated, and the toes were unusually short and seemed strangely small for his feet. I remembered having seen similar symptoms during a brief stint of clinical work I had done several years earlier. No doubt it was very difficult for this man to walk, and it was now apparent why so much of his time was spent sitting. He had leprosy.

Some time after this I again stopped to say hello to him. He smiled as he returned my greeting and appeared glad to see me. We spoke easily now, he in his broken English, and I in my fractured Nepali. Out of respect I now called him *daju*, or "older brother," as was the custom. The first time I did this his expression did not change, but from then on he called me *bhai*, or "younger brother," as though he had been doing so for years.

I cannot explain the feeling, but there has always been something exquisitely heartwarming about being referred to as *bhai* or *daju* by the Nepalis. Perhaps these words were intended to convey nothing more than simple courtesy to a foreigner, but countless times I have been struck by the intimacy these words implied, and the genuine affection with which they were spoken.

We talked for a few more minutes, and when I left I gave him a couple of cigarettes wrapped in a five-rupee note. He accepted this graciously and with dignity. I said good-bye, but resolved to continue to see him until I had to leave.

This I did, and in the course of my last few days in Kathmandu we would talk frequently. I would do as much as I could manage in Nepali, but we usually relied considerably more on English. We sometimes had a glass of tea together in the pale afternoon sun, limiting our conversation to superficial things, but enjoying it nevertheless.

It starts to get cold in November, and prior to leaving I wanted to bring the old man a pair of heavy woolen socks that I had brought for use in the mountains. On my last night in Nepal, I found him sitting in his usual place. It was very cold. I approached him and said that tomorrow I was leaving. I then said that I wished to give him my socks. He said nothing. I felt awkward, but as gently as I could I lifted the blanket that covered his legs. I put the socks on what remained of his feet and tried to explain that I would be pleased if he would keep them.

For a long moment he did not speak. I feared that I might have made him uncomfortable, but then he looked at me with marvelous compassion in his eyes and said, "God bless you, *bhai*. No one has touched me in a very long time."

Robert J. Matthews has made several visits to Nepal and has been featured in a wide range of publications and anthologies from *The Gift of Travel* to *Houghton Mifflin's Thematic Approach to Writing*. He has taught mathematics and humanities-based literature for several years and lives with his wife, Elley, in Marin County, California.

Home Is a Place in Time

PAUL GRUCHOW

What if one's life were not a commodity, not something to be bartered to the highest bidder, or made to order? What if one's life were governed by needs more fundamental than acceptance or admiration? What if one were simply to stay home and plant some manner of garden?

To plant a garden is to enter the continuum of time. Each seed carries in its genome the history that will propel it into the future, and in planting it we stretch one of the long threads of our culture into tomorrow.

A home, like a garden, exists as much in time as in space. A home is the place in the present where one's past and one's future come together, the crossroads between history and heaven. I learned this truth the day we buried my mother.

In the previous month, I had felt often like a man without an anchor. We were living in St. Paul and expecting our first child. For my wife it was a difficult and somewhat dangerous pregnancy. Christmas passed and the days turned toward the new year. The baby was overdue. In those same days, Mother was lying in a hospital bed in Montevideo, Minnesota, emaciated and in pain. She had already lost a brave battle against cancer but was unwilling, just yet, to concede defeat, for reasons that were, to me, mysterious. She was long past delusion about her prospects. My own heart resided in both places, full of fear and hope at the same time. I did not know where my body should be.

On the penultimate day of the old year, the baby, after a stubborn resistance of her own, finally came. She was big and beautiful and healthy. She gave one lusty cry as she entered the world and then lay quietly while she was bathed and dressed, looking about the room in wide-eyed wonder.

I telephoned Mother with the news. She said with surprising energy that she hoped she might see the baby before she died. But that day a fierce cold front had settled over Minnesota. For more than a week, daytime temperatures did not rise above zero. We were, as I suppose first-time parents always are, terrified of our responsibilities. The baby seemed so helpless and fragile. We did not dare risk the three-hour drive to the hospital.

One cloudy morning in mid-January the weather at last broke. We bundled up the baby and made a dash for Montevideo. In the darkened hospital room, we introduced grandmother and granddaughter. The baby slept against the rails of the bed while Mother fondled her with eyes too small for their bony sockets. They joined hands, the baby's soft, fat, and warm, Mother's cold, gaunt, and hard. With tremendous effort, Mother whispered three words barely audible above the hum of the humidifier.

"Is she healthy?" she asked. We wept, because she was.

When we arrived back home, the telephone was ringing. A nurse was on the line with the word, hardly news, that Mother had died.

The weather was still bitter and gray the day we buried her in the little cemetery at St. John's Lutheran Church. After the ceremony the three children—Kathy, Paulette, and I—who felt strangely like children again that day, vulnerable and bewildered in an impossibly big world, took refuge one last time in the farmhouse where we had laughed and cried, together and alone, so many times.

We had meant to see to the household goods. There would not be many other opportunities for it; we lived at a distance from one another and seldom found ourselves together. But almost the first items we came across were the photo albums.

We sat in the living room then, not bothering to light the lamp, looking at the pictures and talking until the day died.

"Do you remember when Mother turned toward the back seat of the car and said, 'Where's your sister?' and Paul said, 'Oh, she fell out a long time ago,' and she *had?*"

"Do you remember the day Mother told the neighbor she couldn't go to the Women's Christian Temperance Union meeting because her wine was ready for bottling?"

"Do you remember the day Kathy fell through the outhouse hole?"

"Do you remember the day you rode your bicycle down the driveway with no hands and it made me so mad I stomped the spokes out of my bicycle's wheels?"

"Do you remember the time we floated a pound of butter in Mother's hot laundry starch?"

Do you remember?

Do you remember?

The stories tumbled as if out of an overstuffed closet. Sometimes we had three of them going at once. We laughed until we ached. I remember it now as one of the happiest afternoons of my life, the metamorphosis of a friendship deepening as the years pass and we three face our own mortalities. I think that I have never been more exactly at home, more tenaciously alive, than that afternoon, when old joy and new sorrow and present love reverberated together inside me.

All history is ultimately local and personal. To tell what we remember, and to keep on telling it, is to keep the past alive in the present. Should we not do so, we could not know, in the deepest sense, how to inhabit a place. To inhabit a place means literally to have made it a habit, to have made it the custom and ordinary practice of our lives, to have learned how to wear a place like a familiar garment, like the garments of sanctity that nuns once wore. The word habit, in its now-dim original form, meant *to own*. We own places not because we possess the deeds to them, but because they have entered the continuum of our lives. What is strange to us—unfamiliar—can never be home.

It is the fashion just now to disparage nostalgia. Nostalgia, we believe, is a cheap emotion. But we forget what it means. In its Greek roots it means, literally, the return to home. It came into currency as a medical word in nineteenth-century Germany to describe the failure to thrive of the displaced persons, including my own ancestors, who had crowded into that country from the east. Nostalgia is the clinical term for homesickness, for the desire to be rooted in a place—to know clearly, that is, what time it is. This desire need not imply the impulse to turn back the clock, which of course we cannot do. It recognizes, rather, the truth—if home is a place in time—that we cannot know where we are now unless we can remember where we have come from.

Paul Gruchow is the author of several books, including *Journal of a Prairie Year, The Necessity of Empty Places,* and *Grass Roots: The Universe of Home,* from which this story was excerpted.

Mother Teresa on Death Row

MICHAEL WAYNE HUNTER

In the summer of 1987, I had just finished my third year on San Quentin's death row. Warehoused on the old death row, or "the shelf" as we call it.

On this particular day, I came onto the tier at 8:30 A.M. on my way to work out with my friend Bobby Harris. After lifting weights for a while, I was off to my cell to change into gym shorts to play basketball.

As I sat on the tier, double-tying my shoes, the guard on the gun rail came down and asked what I was doing.

"What does it look like?" I asked him. "I'm getting ready to go rock up on the roof." That's where the shelf's exercise yard is located, right next to the gas chamber exhaust stack. (Nothing like a daily reality check, you know.) "That's what I do every day after I lift weights," I added.

"You're going to miss Mother Teresa," the guard said. "She's coming today to see you guys."

I looked at him with a cynical smile. "You cops will do anything to keep from running us to the yard, won't you?" I said.

"I'm not missing my sunshine. If she shows, tell her to lace up some high tops and meet me on the roof. I can post her up to the hoop, probably, and shoot over the top of her."

"O.K.," the guard said. "But don't say I didn't warn you." Then he turned and walked away.

Whereupon a couple of alarm bells went off in my head. The guard, I told myself, had given up too easily. Maybe Mother Teresa was coming. Then I thought, "Get real, Hunter." And I finished getting ready to rock, heading up to the roof with everyone else.

But afterward, walking down the stairs back inside, I heard the guard on the gun rail call: "Don't go into your cells and lock up. Mother Teresa stayed to see you guys, too."

So I jogged up to the front in gym shorts and a tattered basketball shirt with the arms ripped out, and on the other side of the security screen was this tiny woman who looked 100 years old. Yes, it was Mother Teresa.

You have to understand that, basically, I'm a dead man. I don't have to observe any sort of social convention; and as a result, I can break all the rules, say what I want.

But one look at this Nobel Prize winner, this woman so many people view as a living saint, and I was speechless.

Incredible vitality and warmth came from her wizened, piercing eyes. She smiled at me, blessed a religious medal, and handed it to me. I wouldn't have walked voluntarily to the front of the tier to see the Warden, the Governor, the President, the Pope. I could not care less about them. But standing before this woman, all I could say was, "Thank you, Mother Teresa."

Then I stepped back to let another dead man come forward to receive his medal.

As I stood there looking at the medal, I knew my wife was going to treasure it. After all, in her youth, she seriously considered becoming a nun. It occurred to me that her sister was going to be absolutely jealous. Perhaps, I thought, I should try to get a second medal.

Taking a chance, I walked the few steps back and asked Mother Teresa for a medal for my sister-in-law. She smiled, blessed one, and handed it to me. Once again, the warmth of her presence surrounded me, then Mother Teresa turned and pointed her hand at the sergeant on the shelf. "What you do to these men," she told him, "you do to God." The sergeant almost faded away in surprise and wonder....

That night, as I wrote my wife and sister-in-law and sent their medals, I told them I couldn't help reflecting on how this woman had chosen to live her life and what she had accomplished, and how I in contrast had just thrown my life away. It was a humbling experience.

So Mother Teresa came and went. The sergeant was affected by her words for a whole day and a half....

My wife, who is also named Teresa (though I call her Terri) started wearing the medal on a chain around her neck. It became one of her prized possessions.

As time went by, however, I began to forget how powerful I had found Mother Teresa's presence. Usually, in talking about her visit, I would just joke that she kept the sarge at bay for thirty-six hours.

Then, in 1989, my fifth year on death row, my wife told me that she couldn't remain married any longer. It was one of the toughest experiences of my life, right up there with when my mother died. Terri told me that she still loved me, but being married to a dead man was just too difficult. We divorced shortly after my death-penalty appeal was rejected by the California Supreme Court. I was at my lowest ebb emotionally. This is when I began to recall the strength and warmth I had felt in Mother Teresa's presence.

I wrote to Terri and asked if I could borrow the religious medal that Mother Teresa had blessed for me.

The medal would be hers, of course. I just wanted to borrow it to recapture some strength from that remarkable woman. I would return the medal when I left death row, probably upon my execution.

Terri sent it to me with a chain, telling me she did not wear it anymore. Since our divorce, Terri had started wearing my wedding band (the one I had worn during our marriage and returned to Terri) on a chain around her neck instead. It made her feel closer to me, Terri said. But she did not miss San Quentin or walking past the gas chamber to see me each week. We began to correspond regularly again, and Terri, through her letters, has become very much a part of my life once more.

Now I wear Mother Teresa's medal every day. I feel linked by it to both the woman who blessed it and the woman who wore it during marriage. It continues to lend me strength in my darkest moments.

Michael Wayne Hunter was a condemned prisoner at San Quentin, who is now serving a life term in prison at Pleasant Valley State Prison, Coalinga. This piece first appeared in *Catholic Digest* and was reprinted in *Prison Life*, and *The Ultimate Journey*.

Yet Lost for Other Causes

JANET GRACE RIEHL

Fate decreed that I fall in love with, but not marry, a black man whose roots were in Ghana. After years of tussling over the question of a shared future, we could never make the dice roll "marriage." A portion of the force rolling the dice on the side of parting, rather than marrying, was the position taken—without collusion—by both sets of parents living on two entirely different continents.

"Scruffy," so nicknamed by his classmates for the way his hair stood up, took me to visit his family just once. His mother was particularly unhappy to have her son bring a white woman home. One of Scruffy's cousins had married a German woman. They'd moved to Europe and made two babies before the marriage broke in divorce. Mixed-race marriages and mixed-race babies made things more complex. Making a life together was hard enough without such an added complication.

Still, I was excited to meet the two people who had conceived and reared the man I loved. I dressed carefully for the visit to his family choosing an ankle-length wraparound skirt made of purple print Ghanaian cloth. I loved the Indonesian wax print, but had given no thought to wearing a slip underneath the single thickness of cloth. On top I wore a white flower-printed blouse borrowed from my best friend, a lady who hailed from Florida. Unfortunately, she wasn't with me to help me dress for the big day, and Scruffy somehow just didn't think to check what my cloth would look like when I moved into the light. In spite of my grandmother's best efforts when I was a teenager to warn me of what happened to loose women who didn't wear slips, I'd never paid that much attention to the underpinnings of my garments after I left the crinoline stage of the 1950s. Since I'd been in Ghana my women friends in the villages only wore two-yard pieces of cloth for waist wrappers as skirts with nothing underneath. I didn't know then that well-brought-up Ghanaian women from the middle classes routinely sewed in fabric liners as a second layer underneath both top and bottom sections of their outfits.

As I stepped into the sunlight in the parlor at Scruffy's parents, anyone who cared to look, could see that beneath my cloth I walked on two legs. With the slightest bit of imagination, one could also guess what lay at the pelvic valley where my legs came together.

His mother's fear that her son's future was in peril fueled the vehemence of her position. She pulled Scruffy aside during the visit to hiss this warning in his ear: "Tell your woman—" here she paused scornfully for effect. I know, because Scruffy told me in the exact tones his mother poured into his ear. "Tell your woman to line her cloth with a wrapper." The implication was clear. To Scruffy's mother, I was none other than a loose white woman— just short of whoredom—hell-bent on leading her son to ruin.

My parents were amazingly broadminded and accepted my unconventional friendship, within certain limits. My mother and father came to visit me in Botswana where I had found work after leaving the Peace Corps in Ghana. As we walked in matching peaceful strides down a red dirt road, my father reminded me of a quote from our old minister. "The good Reverend used to say that we want Negroes for brothers, but not brothers-in-law." There it was, out in the open. Our strides broke and I cried. We argued, turned around, and dropped the subject.

On their way back to the United States, my parents stopped in Ghana where Scruffy hosted and guided them for several days in a wonderful demonstration of Ghanaian hospitality. He met them at the airport, found a taxi, a good hotel, made sure all their needs and wants were met.

They all three liked each other and exchanged presents at visit's end. My father gave Scruffy one of the small dogs he carves from black walnut taken from our own trees. Scruffy chose a sand-cast gold weight for his gift because Ghana is famous for these from the days when it earned its name "Gold Coast." This gold weight still reposed in my mother's china cabinet years later when Scruffy came to visit.

Back in America, my father wrote me of their visit with Scruffy. He understood now what I loved about him. He felt sorry it seemed a love destined not to run the conventional course of marriage, home, and children. In his letter, he enclosed a beautiful poem he'd found. A copy of this poem no doubt exists in one of my lost journals. To this day I don't know the title or author. If only I did! Only one line, the last, never leaves my mind. The remaining mental fragments of the poem go something like this:

> Each together, yet apart
> Bound by mystic laws of twos.
> An interlude, a life vignette,
> Resplendent in its yearning yet
> Lost for other causes.

It was the poem my father sent filled with his compassion for me in this, my first major heartbreak, which brought the force of his love home to me. We might argue. We might never agree on certain points, but I was his daughter—his youngest—whom he wished to shield and protect.

My father, being of the old school, would have died before ever saying "I love you, Janet." I had puzzled over this fact with Scruffy and sometimes suffered from it. Scruffy advised me to smell the love under my nose. When I sniffed the fragrance of my father's gift of words, I identified one more scent of love to file away for future reference. My father's love smelled of pine pitch, mud after rain, and iodine on an open wound. But it was love all the same, and would have to do.

Janet Grace Riehl is a Northern California writer, artist, and creativity coach who operates Rocking Triangle Studio. Her short stories, personal essays, poems, and artwork have been widely published in national literary magazines such as *Cream City Review* and *Harvard Review.*

The Sewing Machine Man

SYLVIA BOORSTEIN

I needed my sewing machine fixed, and since I had moved to a new town I found the local dealer in the Yellow Pages. As I drove up, I noticed a sign in the shop window: "Business is fine. People are terrific. Life is wonderful!" This is an unusual sign for a sewing machine store. It's an unusual sign for any store.

Inside, I found that the walls and countertops were decorated with similar upbeat slogans, the kind I see in key chain catalogs: "When Life Hands You Lemons, Make Lemonade!" "This Day Is What You Received, What You Make Of It Is Up To You." The proprietor of the store acknowledged my presence but stayed totally attentive to his customer. He wasn't rushing, so neither was I.

When it was my turn, he was completely helpful. When we had finished my sewing machine business, I ventured a personal, psychologist's remark: "You seem like a very good-mood person," I said. "Was you mother a cheerful person?"

"No," he responded. "My mother was an alcoholic and very depressed."

"I suppose," I continued, "that you father was a good role model for you."

"No. My father had rage attacks, and he beat us up a lot."

"It's a wonder," I exclaimed, "that you turned out so well!"

"I didn't turn out well at all! I was a mess!" he smiled ruefully. "I did terribly in school. I never really learned to read. I got through high school because I got bigger and bigger, so they moved me along."

He didn't seem to mind telling his story, and I continued to ask questions. His situation defied all conventional wisdom.

"After high school things got worse. I did drugs. I got into trouble. Finally, I didn't know what else to do, so I joined the Marines. The first day, they gave us all uniforms, and they gave us all haircuts. Six of us got haircuts at the same time. They faced us all toward the back wall, and they clipped everyone's hair. Then they turned all six of us around, at the same time, to face the mirror. I was scared for a minute. I couldn't find myself! There was no one there whose story I knew!"

For me, that was the most important line of his narrative. "There was no one there whose story I knew!" He went on to explain how, having seen that it's all a matter of what story you "own," he decided to have a new story. The old one, he figured, wasn't serving him well.

He finished the Marines, learned machines well enough to get trained in sewing machines as a civilian, married, raised a family, and ran a small, thriving business. He laughingly told me he still hadn't read more than one whole book in his life. People seem to flock to his store, though. Partly, I guess, it's because he is good at fixing sewing machines; however, I think it's mostly because they like being around him. I don't suppose everyone who visits his shop asks as many questions as I did. I think they just intuit that he knows something special.

Sylvia Boorstein teaches mindfulness and leads retreats across the U.S. She is a co-founding teacher (with Jack Kornfield) at the Spirit Rock Meditation Center in Woodacre, California, and a senior leader at the Insight Meditation Society in Barre, Massachusetts. She is also a practicing psychotherapist. This story was excerpted from her book, *It's Easier Than You Think: The Buddhist Way to Happiness.*

The Village Watchman

TERRY TEMPEST WILLIAMS

Stories carved in cedar rise from the deep woods of Sitka. These totem poles are foreign to me, this vertical lineage of clans: Eagle, Raven, Wolf, and Salmon. The Tlingit craftsmen create a genealogy of the earth, a reminder of mentors, that we come into this world in need of proper instruction. I sit on the soft floor of this Alaskan forest and feel the presence of Other.

The totem before me is called "Wolf Pole" by locals. The Village Watchman sits on top of Wolf's head with his knees drawn to his chest, his hands holding them tight against his body. He wears a red-and-black-striped hat. His eyes are direct, deep-set, painted blue. The expression on his face reminds me of a man I loved, a man who was born into this world feet first.

"Breech," my mother told me of her brother's birth. "Alan was born feet first. As a result, his brain was denied oxygen. He is special."

As a child, this information impressed me. I remember thinking fish live underwater. Maybe Alan had gills, maybe he didn't need a face-first gulp of air like the rest of us. His sweet breath of initiation came in time, slowly moving up through the soles of his tiny webbed feet. The amniotic sea he had floated in for nine months delivered him with a fluid memory. He knew something. Other.

Wolf, who resides in the center of this totem, holds the tail of Salmon with his feet. The tongue of Wolf hangs down, blood-red, as do his front paws, black. Salmon, a sockeye, is poised down-river—a swish of a tail and he could be gone, but the clasp of Wolf is strong.

There is a story of a boy who was kidnapped from his village by the Salmon People. He was taken from his family to learn the ways of water. When he returned many years later to his home, he was recognized by his own as a Holy Man privy to mysteries of the unseen world. Twenty years after my uncle's death, I wonder if Alan could have been that boy.

But our culture tells a different story, more alien than those of Tlingit or Haida. My culture calls people of sole-births retarded, handicapped, mentally disabled or challenged. We see them for who they are not, rather than for who they are.

My grandmother, Lettie Romney Dixon, wrote in her journal, "It wasn't until Alan was sixteen months old that a busy doctor cruelly broke the news to us. Others may have suspected our son's limitations but to those of us who loved him so unquestionably, lightning struck without warning. I hugged my sorrow to myself. I felt abandoned and lost. I wouldn't accept the verdict. Then we started the trips to a multitude of doctors. Most of them were kind and explained that our child was like a car without brakes, like an electric wire without insulation. They gave us no hope for a normal life."

Normal. Latin: *normalis; norma*, a rule; conforming with or constituting an accepted standard, model or pattern, especially corresponding to the median or average of a large group in type, appearance, achievement, function, or development.

Alan was not normal. He was unique; one and only; single; sole; unusual; extraordinary; rare. His emotions were not measured, his curiosity not bridled. In a sense, he was wild like a mustang in the desert and, like most wild horses, he was eventually rounded up.

He was unpredictable. He created his own rules and they changed from moment to moment. Alan was twelve years old, hyperactive, mischievous, easily frustrated, and unable to learn in traditional ways. The situation was intensified by his seizures. Suddenly, without warning, he would stiffen like a rake, fall forward and crash to the ground, hitting his head. My grandparents could not keep him home any longer. They needed professional guidance and help. In 1957 they reluctantly placed their youngest child in an institution for handicapped children called the American Fork Training School. My grandmother's heart broke for the second time.

Once again, from her journal: "Many a night my pillow is wet from tears of sorrow and senseless dreaming of 'if things had only been different,' or wondering if he is tucked in snug and warm, if he is well and happy, if the wind still bothers him...."

The wind may have continued to bother Alan, certainly the conditions he was living under were less than ideal, but as a family there was much about his private life we never knew. What we did know was that Alan had an enormous capacity for adaptation. We had no choice but to follow him.

I followed him for years.

Alan was ten years my senior. In my mind, growing up, he was mythic. Everything I was taught not to do, Alan did. We were taught to be polite, to not express displeasure or anger in public. Alan was sheer, physical expression. Whatever was on his mind was vocalized and usually punctuated with colorful speech. We would go bowling as a family on Sundays. Each of us would take our turn, hold the black ball to our chest, take a few steps, swing our arm back, forward, glide, and release—the ball would roll down the alley, hit a few pins, we would wait for the ball to return, and then take our second run. Little emotion was shown. When it was Alan's turn, it was an event. Nothing subtle. His style was Herculean. Big man. Big ball. Big roll. Big bang. Whether it was a strike or a gutter, he clapped his hands, spun around on the floor, slapped his thighs, and cried, "Goddamn! Did you see that one? Send me another ball, sweet Jesus!" And the ball was always returned.

I could always count on my uncle for a straight answer. He was my mentor in understanding that one of the remarkable aspects of being human was to hold opposing views in our mind at once.

"How are you doing?" I would ask.

"Ask me how I am feeling." he answered.

"O.K., how are you feeling?"

"Today? Right now?"

"Yes."

"I am very happy and very sad."

"How can you be both at the same time?" I asked in all seriousness, a girl of nine or ten.

"Because both require each other's company. They live in the same house. Didn't you know?"

We would laugh and then go on to another topic. Talking to my uncle was always like entering a maze of riddles. Ask a question. Answer with a question and see where it leads you.

My younger brother Steve and I spent a lot of time with Alan. He offered us shelter from the conventionality of a Mormon family. At our home during Christmas, he would direct us in his own nativity plays. "More—" he would say to us, making wide gestures with his hands. "Give me more of yourself." He was not like anyone we knew. In a culture where we were taught socially to be seen, not heard, Alan was our mirror. We could be different, too. His unquestioning belief in us as children, as human beings, was in startling contrast to the way we saw the public react to him. It hurt us. What we could never tell was if it hurt him.

Each week Steve and I would accompany our grandparents south to visit Alan. It was an hour's drive to the training school from Salt Lake City, mostly through farmlands.

We would enter the grounds, pull into the parking lot of the institution where a playground filled with huge papier-mâché storybook figures stood (a twenty-foot pied piper, a pumpkin carriage with Cinderella inside, the old woman who lived in a shoe), and nine out of ten times, Alan would be standing outside his dormitory waiting for us. We would get out of the car and he would run toward us, throwing his powerful arms around us. His hugs cracked my back and at times I had to fight for my breath. My grandfather would calm him down by simply saying, "We're here, son. You can relax now."

Alan was a formidable man now in his early twenties, stocky and strong. His head was large with a protruding forehead that bore many scars, a line-by-line history of seizures. He always had on someone else's clothes—a tweed jacket too small, brown pants too big, a striped golf shirt that didn't match. He showed us appearances didn't matter, personality did. If you didn't know him, he could look frightening. It was an unspoken rule in our family that the character of others was gauged in how they treated him. The only thing consistent about his attire was that he always wore a silver football helmet from Olympus High School where my grandfather was coach. It was a loving, practical solution to protect Alan when he fell. Quite simply, the helmet cradled his head and absorbed the shock of the seizures.

"Part of the team," my grandfather Sanky would say as he slapped him affectionately on the back. "You're a Titan, son, and I love you—you're a real player on our team."

The windows to the dormitory were dark, reflecting Mount Timpanogos to the east. It was hard to see inside, but I knew what the interior held. It looked like an abandoned gymnasium without bleachers, filled with hospital beds. The stained white walls and yellow-waxed floors offered no warmth to its residents. The stench was nauseating, sweat and urine trapped in the oppression of stale air. I recall the dirty sheets, the lack of privacy, and the almond-eyed children who never rose from their beds. And then I would turn around and face Alan's cheerfulness, the open and loving manner in which he would introduce me to his friends, the pride he exhibited as he showed me around his home. I kept thinking, *Doesn't he see how bad this is, how poorly they are being treated?* His words would return to me, "I am very happy and I am very sad."

For my brother and me, Alan was our guide, our elder. He was fearless. But neither one of us will ever be able to escape the image of Alan kissing his parents good-bye after an afternoon with family and slowly walking back to his dormitory. Before we drove away, he would turn toward us, take off his silver helmet, and wave. The look on his face haunts me still. Alan walked point for all of us.

Alan liked to talk about God. Perhaps it was in these private conversations that our real friendship was forged.

"I know Him," he would say when all the adults were gone.

"You do?" I asked.

"I talk to Him every day."

"How so?"

"I talk to Him in prayers. I listen and then I hear His voice."

"What does He tell you?"

"He tells me to be patient. He tells me to be kind. He tells me that He loves me."

In Mormon culture, children are baptized a member of the Church of Jesus Christ of Latter-Day Saints when they turn eight years old. Alan had never been baptized because my grandparents believed it should be his choice, not something simply taken for granted. When he turned twenty-two, he expressed a sincere desire to join the Church. A date was set immediately.

The entire Dixon clan convened in the Lehi Chapel, a few miles north of the group home where Alan was now living. We were there to support and witness his conversion. As we walked toward the meeting house where this sacred rite was to be performed, Alan had a violent seizure. My grandfather and Uncle Don, Alan's elder brother, dropped down with him, holding his head and body as every muscle thrashed on the pavement like a school of netted fish brought on deck. I didn't want to look, but to walk away would have been worse. We stayed with him, all of us.

"Talk to God," I heard myself saying under my breath. "I love you, Alan."

"Can you hear me, darling?" It was my grandmother's voice, her hand holding her son's head.

By now, many of us were gathered on our knees around him, our trembling hands on his rigid body.

Alan opened his eyes. "I want to be baptized," he said. The men helped him to his feet. The gash on his left temple was deep. Blood dripped down the side of his face. He would forgo stitches once again. My mother had her arm around my grandmother's waist. Shaken, we all followed him inside.

Alan's father and brother ministered to him, stopped the bleeding and bandaged the pressure wound, then helped him change into the designated white garments for baptism. He entered the room with great dignity and sat on the front pew with a dozen or more eight-year-old children seated on either side. Row after row of family sat behind him.

"Alan Romney Dixon." His name was called by the presiding bishop. Alan rose from the pew and met his brother Don, also dressed in white, who took his hand and led him down the blue-tiled stairs into the baptismal font filled with water. They faced the congregation. Don raised his right arm to the square in the gesture of a holy oath as Alan placed his hands on my brother's left forearm. The sacred prayer was offered in the name of the

Father, the Son, and the Holy Ghost, after which my uncle put his right hand behind Alan's shoulder and gently lowered him into the water for a complete baptism by immersion.

Alan emerged from the holy waters like an angel.

Six years later, I found myself sitting in a chair across from my uncle at the University Hospital, where he was being treated for a severe ear infection. I was eighteen; he was twenty-eight.

"Alan," I asked. "What is it really like to be inside your body?"

He crossed his legs and placed both hands on the arms of the chair. His brown eyes were piercing.

"I can't tell you what it's like except to say I feel pain for not being seen as the person I am."

A few days later, Alan died alone; unique; one and only; single; in American Fork, Utah.

With her first book, *Refuge: An Unnatural History of Family and Place,* Terry Tempest Williams won an immediate reputation as an eloquent and impassioned naturalist writer in the traditions of John Muir, Rachel Carson, and Wallace Stegner. Her books since then have included *The Open Space of Democracy, Red: Passion and Patience in the Desert, Leap, Pieces of White Shell: A Journey to Navajoland, Coyote's Canyon,* and *An Unspoken Hunger: Stories from the Field.* She lives in Salt Lake City with her husband, Brooke

A Powerful Gesture

DIANE RIGDA

They rise, dignified and silent, behind neon hotel signs and stoplights lining the main strip leading to Giza. Egypt's pyramids represent an icon of antiquity, and are astonishing to behold. The pyramids, however, are not what I remember best about Cairo.

I had come to Cairo to glimpse those famed structures, which for millennia have drawn countless pilgrims, but I was in the region because I wanted to learn about the culture and people of the Middle East. I had studied Arabic and had already been through Syria and Jordan, where I was showered with that very genuine Arabian hospitality.

By the time I got to Cairo, I knew how to ask for the bathroom and could easily navigate a strange city on my own. I was also aware and respectful of the heightened sense of modesty in a place where men and women alike are expected to wear long sleeves and headscarves

I took public transport around the city. Though taxis were cheap and easy, I enjoyed the challenge of deciphering the maze of trams. It forced me to practice my Arabic and enjoy the abundant helpfulness of Cairenes.

Each tram had a women's car, which was where I usually rode, but during rush hour one sweltering June day, I found no space in the women's car. I stood near an open window and hung on, careful not to look at or touch any of the men swaying nearby. My long black skirt trapped the heat to my dripping legs and my cotton scarf kept the Cairo grime out of my auburn hair and the sun off my face.

We lurched, rumbled along, stopped. People stepped down and others climbed on. In my heat-induced reverie, I gazed out the window and daydreamed of what I would eat for dinner and the sweat trails on my thighs.

In spite of my inattention, I suddenly sensed a pair of eyes on me. I glanced up and saw a leering man removing my skirt and blouse with his eyes. In any culture, this was a stare that violated. I ignored him, but he continued his silent assault. I pulled my cotton scarf completely over my face hiding every bit of exposed skin. I couldn't see him but knew that he enjoyed this bullying.

I hated the heat, despised the leering man, and wanted off the tram, but I stubbornly stayed put. In the Middle East, no sane Arabian man would stare at an Arabian woman, because her escort would see to it that the offender thoroughly regretted the act. As a foreigner, I was an easy victim for this opportunist, this coward.

Suddenly, there was a stir around me. Harsh words hurled at my attacker. I couldn't understand the rapid colloquialisms, but it was clear what had happened. The men around us had witnessed our pas de deux and come to my defense.

My fellow passengers, all men, yelled this man, this leering creep, off the tram. Appropriately shamed, he got off at the next stop. I said nothing, looked at no one. My gratitude couldn't even show in a smile but they knew I appreciated it. I could have removed my scarf, my blouse, my skirt, and no one would have looked.

A simple gesture by living humans upstaged those remarkable pyramids for me forever.

Diane Rigda has traveled extensively in the Middle East and parts of Africa, but she still enjoys the low-key public transit of San Francisco, where she lives.

Do You Love the Boy?

MAYA ANGELOU

When I was sixteen, a boy in high school evinced interest in me, so I had sex with him—just once. And after I came out of that room, I thought, *Is that all there is to it?* My goodness, I'll never do that again! Then, when I found out I was pregnant, I went to the boy and asked him for help, but he said it wasn't his baby and he didn't want any part of it.

I was scared to pieces. Back then, if you had money, there were some girls who got abortions, but I couldn't deal with that idea. Oh, no. No. I knew there was somebody inside me. So I decided to keep the baby.

My older brother, Bailey, my confidant, told me not to tell my mother or she'd take me out of school. So I hid it the whole time with big blouses! Finally, three weeks before I was due, I left a note on my stepfather's pillow telling him I was pregnant. He told my mother, and when she came home, she calmly asked me to run her bath.

I'll never forget what she said: "Now tell me this—do you love the boy?" I said no. "Does he love you?" I said no. "Then there's no point in ruining three lives. We are going to have our baby!"

What a knockout she was as a mother of teens. Very loving.

Very accepting. Not one minute of recrimination. And I never felt any shame.

I'm telling you that the best decision I ever made was keeping that baby! Yes, absolutely. Guy was a delight from the start—so good, so bright, and I can't imagine my life without him.

At seventeen I got a job as a cook and later as a nightclub waitress. I found a room with cooking privileges, because I was a woman with a baby and needed my own place. My mother, who had a fourteen-room house, looked at me as if I was crazy! She said, "Remember this: You can always come home." She kept that door open. And every time life kicked me in the belly, I would go home for a few weeks.

I struggled, sure. We lived hand-to-mouth, but it was really heart-to-hand. Guy had love and laughter and a lot of good reading and poetry as a child. Having my son brought out the best in me and enlarged my life. Whatever he missed, he himself is a great father today. He was once asked what it was like growing up in Maya Angelou's shadow, and he said, "I always thought I was in her light."

Years later, when I was married, I wanted to have more children, but I couldn't conceive. Isn't it wonderful that I had a child at sixteen? Praise God!

At age three, after the dissolution of her parents' marriage, poet, playwright, and director Maya Angelou was raised, until age fourteen, in Stamps, Arkansas, by her paternal grandmother. Angelou's eloquent series of five memoirs includes *I Know Why the Caged Bird Sings* and *A Song Flung Up to Heaven.*

Big Sur and Starting Over

PAUL WINSTON

I had slogged my way through the paperwork and preliminaries, and suddenly we owned a large chunk of a Big Sur ranch on an isolated, oceanfront slice of the central California coast.

Now what? My partner, a brilliant and successful designer, said: "I'll design a house for you and another one for my wife and me. You'll leave the business world and write books"—my stated dream—"and I'll get out of designing furniture and learn to paint," which was his stated dream.

So much for stated dreams. You do have to be careful what you dream, should they come true. For all the wrong reasons, my dreams lay far afield from where I was at this hour of my life. I knew nothing of hotels or restaurants. "Bloom where you are planted," said a motto on a friend's bulletin board. So that's what I did. Of course, my partner went on to paint beautiful pictures that sold like hotcakes. I wrote one book. I now use the back pages of the manuscript for scratch paper.

On the highway where our ranch began was a small café, a gas station, and a campground. I quickly became a pumper of gas, a cook or a waiter when we were desperate, and absolutely useless in the campground, where a kid half my age ran it superbly.

But then a huge rainstorm sent a mudslide down our mountains and blocked the road. Our cook, Fern, could not get to work, so I was recruited to go into the kitchen that morning.

"Oh, I can do that," I thought. A bunch of orders of ham and eggs suddenly came in from the road-repair crew. I flipped one fried egg just the way I'd seen our cook do it when I was a little boy. It flew high into the air and then slipped behind the stove, onto the floor. I think it stayed there until we tore down the café years later to build our new hotel and restaurant.

Our waitress, Samantha, finally strode into the kitchen a few minutes later, after I'd told her we were all out of fried eggs and only had scrambled eggs. She announced that a patron was standing on a chair, pinching the edge of a cremated egg between his fingers and demanding to know—at the top of his voice—if we expected him to pay for his breakfast.

Samantha gave me her order book and apron and took over cooking. I took over taking orders. By the fourth day, I wasn't bad. People said they liked my wisecracks as I served them. They laughed at my lines.

Then one day a young man entered, dressed in a pinstriped dark suit and wingtip shoes—the whole banker's uniform—very much out of place, sartorially, among our cowboy clientele.

"The soup is good today," I said, shoving a menu toward him. "Vegetable noodle. You'll like it."

He nodded, and I wrote it down, adding expectantly, "And then...?"

"That's all I have time for," he replied. "I'm playing hooky from my job today, just exploring this beautiful coast. You're fortunate to live here. What's it like?" I started my glowing replies until I looked at his face and realized he was the one who wanted to talk. Later, after he'd finished his soup, he complimented it and began telling me a story.

"Look, this Big Sur is the most beautiful place I've ever seen," he began. "Uh, I was just wondering if you had a job you could give me if I come back in a few weeks. I'll dig ditches, anything at all."

"No," I replied, "that's the vice-president's job. He's worse at it than I was, but fortunately we don't need a lot of ditches dug just now."

Then it all poured out. His wife was leaving him, taking the kids. He hated his job, even though he was already the youngest vice-president at a huge American corporation near Chicago. He felt he had no one who cared, nowhere to turn, and by the time he'd finished our great soup, he said, he'd decided: He wanted to make a clean break from the past and move to Big Sur.

I looked at his shoes.

"You'll last one week here," I said.

"I've got exactly one pair of jeans and some work boots, and I'll do anything you say. I'll work hard." I started to shake my head. The stranger quickly added, "My dad was an admiral. I went to Annapolis but didn't do well there. I never wanted that life, but I was trying to make him proud of me, and so I...."

He ran out of gas. So that was it. Why hadn't he just said so? I was an honors graduate from the school of trying-to-make-Dad-proud-of-me. Empathy swept over me. I stopped shaking my head. I nodded it. He shook my hand, smiled broadly, and drove away in his corporate rent-a-car. Oh well, I thought; we'll never see him again.

He pulled up again three weeks later, in an old car towing a small trailer that held all his worldly possessions, as he put it. He was wearing jeans and work boots. What could I do? We put him to work. We gave him the hardest and least attractive chores. How long could a well-educated, almost-former-military officer, who had a bright career as vice president of a prestigious corporation last in Big Sur?

The answer: quite a while.

Ten years later, I sold the hotel and moved away, but I heard years after I left that he was still there, with his new wife (one of our former waitresses) and their family. He had founded his own local company, which made art products. No one ever worked harder for us, or served us more faithfully. He was a fine person in every way, someone who had awakened to discover new sources of happiness. He became a pillar of our tiny community. It was a privilege to know him.

Yes, but how did I know that on the day I'd served him soup and nodded my head? The answer is, I didn't know that. Listening helps; I just did as I was told.

The other thing I did was to continue to stay out of the way most of the time. And you know what? Our place became a huge success.

Paul Winston grew up in Beverly Hills, the son of Jewish immigrants who fled Tsarist Russia in the 1890s, walking by night from Kiev to Hamburg, then traveling by boat to New York and by train to California. He attended the University of Southern California, followed by Harvard Law School, and a Rhodes Scholarship nomination. His essays have appeared in *The Ultimate Journey: Inspiring Stories of Living and Dying, The Christian Science Monitor,* and other publications. For much of his life he has been involved in the luxury hotel business, and he was last seen by the editors in County Wicklow, Ireland, working on a new resort project.

The Richest Gift

Richard Sterling

I was still quite a young GI, but I had had a full combat tour in Vietnam, and that was more than enough, when in April of 1975 I was sent back in as a member of the expeditionary force tasked with extracting the South Vietnamese government, their dependents, and many thousands of fleeing civilians.

All was disorder, and our efforts were reduced to ad lib and impromptu, and I just didn't want to be the last to die in a useless war. In the chaos of bringing people to boats to be sent downriver to safety I saw a young boy of about six. He had been separated from his family and was crying, rather softly in the noise and tumult, as war children will do. I scooped the boy up as we hurried to the docks, hoisted him to my shoulder and he clung to my neck instinctively.

His name was Duk. I kept him close to me throughout the day and into the night as the North Vietnamese army prepared its final assault on the city of Saigon, and we made our way to a ship of the U.S. 7th Fleet lying offshore. There the boy and I stayed together, eating and sleeping and recuperating on the weather decks until late the next day when his family was located on another ship. I carried Duk down the accommodation ladder to a whaleboat. And I felt the need to give him something, a gift of some kind, something of me. I had nothing else, so I took off my cap and placed it on his head. He gave me a little soldier's salute, and I sent him reluctantly off to his future.

Fast forward fifteen years to summer. At a company picnic, by fate or by breathtaking coincidence, I met a young man who turned out to be "the boy." Duk was an inch taller than I, dangerously handsome, and he told me that he had just graduated from Stanford University. And that my cap still hangs on the wall in his room.

I've never had a richer gift.

Richard Sterling is the author of *The Fire Never Dies, How to Eat Around the World,* and a number of books in the Lonely Planet World Food Series. His anthology *Food* won a Lowell Thomas Award for Best Travel Book, and he is also the editor of *The Adventure of Food.*

The Magic Formula

NEALE DONALD WALSCH

"Helen" was one of ninety-seven participants at a holiday retreat which was held in the mountains of Estes Park, Colorado. On the final night of the retreat before our New Year's Eve resolutions ritual, Helen raised her hand and asked for the microphone. "I've heard a lot this week about how God is our best friend, how God is wonderful and loving, and how we should all have a conversation with God every day," she began. "Well, if had a conversation with God, I would tell Him that I am damned angry with Him."

"That's O.K.," I said, "God can handle that. But are you O.K.?"

"No," she said, and her voice was trembling now.

"Well, just what are you angry with God about?"

Helen took a deep breath. "Almost twenty-five years ago we adopted a baby boy. We had tried to conceive for five years, without success. It looked like we would never be parents. My biological clock was running out. So we adopted Billy. Three weeks later, I discovered I was pregnant. I had the child, another boy, and raised them both as my own, although we did tell our first son when he grew a little older that he was adopted. We wanted to be truthful with him. We told him we loved him exactly the same as his brother, and we knew that our actions showed him that.

"There was never any complication around this until Billy was eight. Then one day he came home from school very angry. They must nave been teasing him on the playground or something. You know how kids can be. They can sometimes be very cruel. Anyway, he came home just furious, and wanted to know why his mommy would give him away. He also demanded to see his mommy right away.

"I felt terrible, of course. First, for the anguish and hurt that I could see Billy was going through, and second for myself. I was filled with sadness because, of course, I felt that I was Billy's mommy. I stood there remembering the nights of changing diapers and nursing him through sickness and all the things that mommies do, and my heart broke that Billy didn't see me anymore as, didn't think of me, as his mom.

"But I understood—I had to understand—and I promised him that when he was older, if he still felt he wanted to, he would meet his mom. I would do whatever I could to find her and arrange it.

"This seemed O.K. with Billy, but he never seemed to get over his anger. He just had this anger all through the rest of his childhood and into his teen years, which were very difficult for us. We all got through it, but it wasn't easy on any of us in the family, and certainly not on me.

"When Billy had grown older, we talked again about seeing his mother, and we made an agreement that when he turned twenty-one, I would begin searching for her if he still wanted me to. Throughout the rest of his teen years he reminded me of that promise. Finally, Billy's twenty-first birthday arrived. Not long after, he was killed in an automobile accident."

There was a collective gasp from the retreat participants. Abruptly, Helen's energy shifted into anger.

"Now I want you to tell me," she snapped, "how any kind of loving God could have let that happen, just when Billy was about to meet his mother, just when we were about to reconcile the strain which his yearning had placed on our relationship. I want you to tell me, why would God do that?"

The room plummeted into stunned silence.

I was stopped cold. I stared at Helen for a moment, then closed my eyes and went within. I heard my thoughts. "O.K., God, this is it. I don't know what to say here. You've got to help me out."

Suddenly, my eyes popped open, my mind overflowing. I spoke the words I heard in my head before I had a chance to judge them or edit them.

"Billy died at twenty-one because that was when he was promised he would meet his mother— and when he turned twenty-one his mother was not on this Earth."

The room gasped again. Someone whispered, "Yes." Someone else cried. I went on.

"There is no such thing as an accident, and nothing happens by coincidence in God's world. You were given a biological son, even though you had not been able to conceive and it looked as if you might never be able to do so, because there was a plan—a larger plan in place. You were given this special gift in exchange for your willingness to take Billy in, give him a home, love him and raise him as your own, and care for him until he was ready to meet his mother, and she was ready to meet him.

"The day of Billy's death was the happiest day of his life. And his gratefulness to you for bringing him to that moment is eternal. It surrounds your heart, and creates with you an everlasting bond. There is perfection in Life's design and in every human circumstance and experience. In every condition. Our opportunity is to notice this. That is also our release, our salvation. The end to our suffering and our pain."

Helen's face changed immediately. Filled with anger just moments before, now it was aglow. Her whole body seemed drained of every tension. She looked relaxed for the first time in a week. And tears ran down her cheeks, even as she smiled with a radiance that filled the room.

I've told this story because I want you to know what Helen and all the other participants in that retreat now know. There is a "magic formula" which has been given to us by the heavens. It is a formula with which all sadness, all anger, all negativity surrounding any human experience is dissolved. It is a formula which allows us to recreate ourselves anew. It is a formula easy to remember, and stated in three words: *See the perfection.*

Ah, but does it work? Does it really work?

New Year's Day, Helen handed me a note. She'd written a poem when she'd returned to her room after a walk under the clear, crisp Colorado sky the night before.

> I came here with a burdened heart,
> A heart afraid to cry.
> It's near three years since Billy left
> And I couldn't say goodbye.
> I stood, alone, beside his grave
> And couldn't even cry.
> We had a deal, I said to him
> You left me high and dry.
> It's near three years since Billy left,
> God had not seen fit to try
> To soothe this hurt, to heal this heart,
> To give me tears to cry
> And then God spoke. He pointed out
> That even though he tried,
> My heart was closed and couldn't hear
> His gentle, ageless sigh.
> And though it was just Neale whose voice

Brought the message from on high,
My spirit heard God's words tonight,
And now my eyes can cry.
I took a walk this starry night.
It's finally time to try
To find the joy to free my son
It's time to say goodbye
And as I did, a shooting star…
…danced across the sky.

Neale Donald Walsch is a modern-day spiritual messenger whose words continue to touch the world in profound ways. Neale was born in Milwaukee, Wisconsin to a Roman Catholic family that encouraged his quest for spiritual truth. With an early interest in religion and a deeply felt connection to spirituality, Neale spent the majority of his life thriving professionally, until he encountered a number of serious personal and financial setbacks. He wrote an angry letter to God detailing his problems and received an unexpected and astounding answer. Thus began his now famous conversation with God. His *With God* series of books has been translated into twenty-seven languages, touching millions of lives and inspiring important changes the lives of countless individuals

The Invitation

ORIAH MOUNTAIN DREAMER

It doesn't interest me what you do for a living.
I want to know what you ache for
and if you dare to dream of meeting your heart's longing.

It doesn't interest me how old you are.
I want to know if you will risk looking like a fool
for love
for your dream
for the adventure of being alive.

It doesn't interest me what planets are squaring your moon ...
I want to know if you have touched the center of your own
sorrow
if you have been opened by life's betrayals
or have become shriveled and closed
from fear of further pain.

I want to know if you can sit with pain
mine or your own
without moving to hide it
or fade it
or fix it.

I want to know if you can be with joy
mine or your own
if you can dance with wildness
and let the ecstasy fill you to the tips of your fingers and toes
without cautioning us to
be careful
be realistic
remember the limitations of being human.

It doesn't interest me if the story you are telling me
is true.
I want to know if you can
disappoint another
to be true to yourself.
If you can bear the accusation of betrayal
and not betray your own soul.
If you can be faithless
and therefore trustworthy.

I want to know if you can see Beauty
even when it is not pretty
every day.
And if you can source your own life
from its presence.

I want to know if you can live with failure
yours and mine
and still stand on the edge of the lake
and shout to the silver of the full moon,
"*Yes.*"

It doesn't interest me to know
where you live or how much money you have.
I want to know if you can get up
after the night of grief and despair
weary and bruised to the bone
and do what needs to be done
to feed the children.

It doesn't interest me who you know
or how you came to be here.
I want to know if you will stand
in the center of the fire
with me
and not shrink back.

It doesn't interest me where or what or with whom
you have studied.
I want to know what sustains you
from the inside
when all else falls away.

I want to know if you can be alone
with yourself
and if you truly like the company you keep
in the empty moments.

Oriah Mountain Dreamer is a teacher and writer living in Toronto. While her family history includes stories of Scottish, German, and Native American descent, she is a Canadian woman, and not an "Indian elder" as has sometimes been reported, being neither old enough nor wise enough to claim the status of "elder" for any people. She has had the privilege of studying with and learning from the wisdom of Native American elders who gave her the medicine name, Mountain Dreamer.

Acknowledgments

We would like to thank our families and friends for their usual forbearance while we are putting a book together. Many thanks also to Susan Brady, Jennifer Leo, Stefan Gutermuth, Melanie Haage, Judy Johnson, Alexandria Brady, for their support and contributions to the book.

"The Physics of Kindness" by Huey D. Johnson reprinted from the December 30, 1998 issue of the *San Francisco Examiner*. Copyright © 1998 by Huey D. Johnson. Reprinted by permission of the author.

"Big Howie" by Donald G. Smith reprinted from the September 9, 1996 issue of the *San Francisco Examiner*. Copyright © 1996 by Donald G. Smith. Reprinted by permission of the author.

"Kurt's View" by Kurt Vonnegut with David H. Freedman excerpted from "Vonnegut and Clancy on Technology" from the December 1995 issue of *Inc. Magazine*. Copyright © 1995.

"The Chair" by Jeffrey Burke excerpted from *Island Lighthouse Inn: A Chronicle* by Jeffrey Burke. Copyright © 1997 by Jeffrey Burke. Reprinted by permission of The Pilgrim Press.

"Peak Experience" by Mark Hawthorne published with permission from the author. Copyright © 2005 by Mark Hawthorne.

"Salvation in a Concentration Camp" by Vicktor E. Frankl excerpted from *Man's Search for Meaning* by Vicktor E. Frankl. Copyright © 1959 by Viktor E. Frankl. Reprinted by permission of Beacon Press.

"Love at First Sight" by Douglas Preston excerpted from *Talking to the Ground: One Family's Journey on Horseback Across the Sacred Land of the Navajo* by Douglas Preston. Copyright © 1995 by Douglas Preston. Reprinted by permission of Simon & Schuster Adult Publishing Group.

"Jimbo" by Rick Bass excerpted from *Oil Notes* by Rick Bass. Copyright © 1989 by Rick Bass. Reprinted by permission of the author.

"Eyes on Another World" by Connie McDougall originally appeared as "Seeing Through an Astronaut's Eyes" in the August 18-24, 1995 issue of *The Christian Science Monitor*. Copyright © 1995 by Connie McDougall. Reprinted by permission of the author.

"A Powerful Gesture" by Diane Rigda published with permission from the author. Copyright © 2005 by Diane Rigda.

"Do You Love the Boy?" by Maya Angelou first published as "The Decision That Changed My Life: Keeping My Baby" in the October 9, 2002 issue of *Family Circle*. Copyright © 2002 by Maya Angelou.

"Big Sur and Starting Over" by Paul Winston first published as "Of Soup, Big Sur, and Starting Over" in the December 15, 1999 issue of *The Christian Science Monitor*. Copyright © 1999 by Paul Winston.

"The Richest Gift" by Richard Sterling published with permission from the author. Copyright © 2005 by Richard Sterling.

"The Magic Formula" by Neale Donald Walsch reprinted from the November/December 2004 issue of *Changing Beliefs: The Newsletter of the New Spirituality*. Copyright © 2004. Reprinted by permission of The Conversations with God Foundation and the author.

"The Invitation" by Oriah Mountain Dreamer excerpted from *The Invitation* by Oriah Mountain Dreamer. Copyright © 1999 by Oriah Mountain Dreamer. Reprinted by permission of HarperCollins Publishers, Inc.

About the Editors

James O'Reilly, president and publisher of Travelers' Tales, was born in England and raised in San Francisco. He graduated from Dartmouth College in 1975 and wrote mystery serials before becoming a travel writer in the early 1980s. He's visited more than forty countries, along the way meditating with monks in Tibet, participating in West African voodoo rituals, living in the French Alps, and hanging out the laundry with nuns in Florence. He travels extensively with his wife, Wenda, and their three daughters. They live in Palo Alto, California, where they also publish art games and books for children at Birdcage Books (www.birdcagebooks.com).

Sean O'Reilly is director of special sales and editor-at-large for Travelers' Tales. He is a former seminarian, stockbroker, and prison instructor with a degree in Psychology. Author of the controversial book on men's behavior, *How to Manage Your DICK*, he is also the inventor of a safety device known as Johnny Upright. Widely traveled, Sean most recently completed a journey through China and Southeast Asia. He lives in Virginia with his wife and six children.

Larry Habegger, executive editor of Travelers' Tales, has been writing about travel since 1980. He has visited almost fifty countries and six of the seven continents, traveling from the Arctic to equatorial rain forests, the Himalayas to the Dead Sea. In the early 1980s he co-authored mystery serials for the *San Francisco Examiner* with James O'Reilly, and since 1985 their syndicated column, "World Travel Watch," has appeared in newspapers in five countries and on WorldTravelWatch.com. As series editors of Travelers' Tales, they have worked on some eighty titles, winning many awards for excellence. Habegger regularly teaches the craft of travel writing at workshops and writers conferences, and he lives with his family on Telegraph Hill in San Francisco.

TRAVELERS' TALES
THE POWER OF A GOOD STORY

New Releases

THE BEST TRAVEL WRITING 2005 $16.95
True Stories from Around the World
Edited by James O'Reilly, Larry Habegger & Sean O'Reilly
The second in a new annual series presenting fresh, lively storytelling and compelling narrative to make the reader laugh, weep, and buy a plane ticket.

IT'S A DOG'S WORLD $14.95
True Stories of Travel with Man's Best Friend
Edited by Christine Hunsicker
Introduction by Maria Goodavage
Hilarious and heart warming stories of traveling with canine companions.

A SENSE OF PLACE $18.95
Great Travel Writers Talk About Their Craft, Lives, and Inspiration
By Michael Shapiro
A stunning collection of interviews with the world's leading travel writers, including: Isabel Allende, Bill Bryson, Tim Cahill, Arthur Frommer, Pico Iyer, Peter Matthiessen, Frances Mayes, Jan Morris, Redmond O'Hanlon, Jonathan Raban, Paul Theroux, Simon Winchester, and many more.

WHOSE PANTIES ARE THESE? $14.95
More Misadventures from Funny Women on the Road
Edited by Jennifer L. Leo
Following on the high heels of the award-winning bestseller *Sand in My Bra and other Misadventures* comes another collection of hilarious travel stories by women.

SAFETY AND SECURITY FOR WOMEN WHO TRAVEL (SECOND EDITION) $14.95
By Sheila Swan & Peter Laufer
"A cache of valuable advice."   —*The Christian Science Monitor*

A WOMAN'S PASSION FOR TRAVEL $17.95
True Stories of World Wanderlust
Edited by Marybeth Bond & Pamela Michael
"A diverse and gripping series of stories!"   —Arlene Blum, author of *Annapurna: A Woman's Place*

THE GIFT OF TRAVEL $14.95
Inspiring Stories from Around the World
Edited by Larry Habegger, James O'Reilly & Sean O'Reilly
"Like gourmet chefs in a French market, the editors of Travelers' Tales pick, sift, and prod their way through the weighty shelves of contemporary travel writing, creaming off the very best."   —William Dalrymple, author of *City of Djinns*

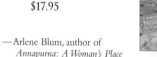

Travel Humor

SAND IN MY BRA AND OTHER MISADVENTURES $14.95
Funny Women Write from the Road
Edited by Jennifer L. Leo
"A collection of ridiculous and sublime travel experiences."
—*San Francisco Chronicle*

LAST TROUT IN VENICE $14.95
The Far-Flung Escapades of an Accidental Adventurer
By Doug Lansky
"Traveling with Doug Lansky might result in a considerably shortened life expectancy . . . but what a way to go."
—Tony Wheeler, Lonely Planet Publications

THERE'S NO TOILET PAPER ON THE ROAD LESS TRAVELED $12.95
The Best of Travel Humor and Misadventure
Edited by Doug Lansky

——— ★ ★ ★ ———
Humor Book of the Year
Independent Publisher's
Book Award

——— ★ ★ ★ ———
ForeWord Gold Medal
Winner—Humor
Book of the Year

HYENAS LAUGHED AT ME AND NOW I KNOW WHY $14.95
The Best of Travel Humor and Misadventure
Edited by Sean O'Reilly, Larry Habegger & James O'Reilly
Hilarious, outrageous and reluctant voyagers indulge us with the best misadventures around the world.

NOT SO FUNNY WHEN IT HAPPENED $12.95
The Best of Travel Humor and Misadventure
Edited by Tim Cahill
Laugh with Bill Bryson, Dave Barry, Anne Lamott, Adair Lara, and many more.

WHOSE PANTIES ARE THESE? $14.95
More Misadventures from Funny Women on the Road
Edited by Jennifer L. Leo
Following on the high heels of the award-winning bestseller *Sand in My Bra and other Misadventures* comes another collection of hilarious travel stories by women.

Travelers' Tales Classics

COAST TO COAST $16.95
A Journey Across 1950s America
By Jan Morris
After reporting on the first Everest ascent in 1953, Morris spent a year journeying across the United States. In brilliant prose, Morris records with exuberance and curiosity a time of innocence in the U.S.

THE ROYAL ROAD TO ROMANCE $14.95
By Richard Halliburton
"Laughing at hardships, dreaming of beauty, ardent for adventure, Halliburton has managed to sing into the pages of this glorious book his own exultant spirit of youth and freedom."
—*Chicago Post*

THE RIVERS RAN EAST
By Leonard Clark
Clark is the original Indiana Jones, telling the breathtaking story of his search for the legendary El Dorado gold in the Amazon.

TRADER HORN $16.95
A Young Man's Astounding Adventures in 19th Century Equatorial Africa
By Alfred Aloysius Horn
Here is the stuff of legends—thrills and danger, wild beasts, serpents, and savages. An unforgettable and vivid portrait of a vanished Africa.

UNBEATEN TRACKS IN JAPAN $14.95
By Isabella L. Bird
Isabella Bird was one of the most adventurous women travelers of the 19th century with journeys to Tibet, Canada, Korea, Turkey, Hawaii, and Japan. A fascinating read.

$16.95

Spiritual Travel

THE SPIRITUAL GIFTS OF TRAVEL $16.95
The Best of Travelers' Tales
Edited by James O'Reilly & Sean O'Reilly
Favorite stories of transformation on the road
that show the myriad ways travel indelibly
alters our inner landscapes.

PILGRIMAGE $16.95
Adventures of the Spirit
Edited by Sean O'Reilly & James O'Reilly
Introduction by Phil Cousineau

ForeWord Silver Medal Winner
— Travel Book of the Year

THE ROAD WITHIN $18.95
True Stories of Transformation
and the Soul
Edited by Sean O'Reilly, James O'Reilly &
Tim O'Reilly

Independent Publisher's Book Award
—Best Travel Book

THE WAY OF THE WANDERER $14.95
Discover Your True Self Through Travel
By David Yeadon
Experience transformation through travel
with this delightful, illustrated collection by
award-winning author David Yeadon.

A WOMAN'S PATH $16.95
Women's Best Spiritual Travel Writing
Edited by Lucy McCauley, Amy G. Carlson &
Jennifer Leo
"A sensitive exploration of women's lives
that have been unexpectedly and spiritually
touched by travel experiences.... Highly
recommended."
—Library Journal

THE ULTIMATE JOURNEY $17.95
Inspiring Stories of Living and Dying
James O'Reilly, Sean O'Reilly & Richard
Sterling
"A glorious collection of writings about the
ultimate adventure. A book to keep by one's
bedside—and close to one's heart."
—Philip Zaleski, editor,
The Best Spiritual Writing series

Special Interest

THE BEST TRAVELERS' TALES 2004 $16.95
True Stories from Around the World
Edited by James O'Reilly, Larry Habegger &
Sean O'Reilly
"This book will grace my bedside for years
to come."
—Simon Winchester, from the Introduction

TESTOSTERONE PLANET $17.95
True Stories from a Man's World
Edited by Sean O'Reilly, Larry Habegger &
James O'Reilly
Thrills and laughter with some of today's best
writers, including Sebastian Junger, Tim Cahill,
Bill Bryson, and Jon Krakauer.

THE GIFT OF TRAVEL $14.95
Inspiring Stories from Around the World
Edited by Larry Habegger, James O'Reilly
& Sean O'Reilly
"Like gourmet chefs in a French market, the
editors of Travelers' Tales pick, sift, and prod
their way through the weighty shelves of
contemporary travel writing, creaming off the
very best."
—William Dalrymple, author of *City of Djinns*

DANGER! $17.95
True Stories of Trouble and Survival
Edited by James O'Reilly, Larry Habegger &
Sean O'Reilly
"Exciting ... for those who enjoy living on
the edge or prefer to read the survival stories
of others, this is a good pick."
—Library Journal

365 TRAVEL $14.95
A Daily Book of Journeys, Meditations, and Adventures
Edited by Lisa Bach
An illuminating collection of travel wisdom and adventures that reminds us all of the lessons we learn while on the road.

THE GIFT OF RIVERS $14.95
True Stories of Life on the Water
Edited by Pamela Michael
Introduction by Robert Hass
"...a soulful compendium of wonderful stories that illuminate, educate, inspire, and delight."
—David Brower,
Chairman of Earth Island Institute

FAMILY TRAVEL $17.95
The Farther You Go, the Closer You Get
Edited by Laura Manske
"This is family travel at its finest."
—*Working Mother*

LOVE & ROMANCE $17.95
True Stories of Passion on the Road
Edited by Judith Babcock Wylie
"A wonderful book to read by a crackling fire." —*Romantic Traveling*

THE GIFT OF BIRDS $17.95
True Encounters with Avian Spirits
Edited by Larry Habegger & Amy G. Carlson
"These are all wonderful, entertaining stories offering a *bird's-eye view!* of our avian friends."
—*Booklist*

IT'S A DOG'S WORLD $14.95
True Stories of Travel with Man's Best Friend
Edited by Christine Hunsicker
Introduction by Maria Goodavage
Hilarious and heart warming stories of traveling with canine companions.

Travel Advice

THE PENNY PINCHER'S PASSPORT TO LUXURY TRAVEL (2ND EDITION) $14.95
The Art of Cultivating Preferred Customer Status
By Joel L. Widzer
Completely updated and revised, this 2nd edition of the popular guide to traveling like the rich and famous without being either describes, both philosophically and in practical terms, how to obtain luxurious travel benefits by building relationships with airlines and other travel companies.

SAFETY AND SECURITY FOR WOMEN WHO TRAVEL (2ND EDITION) $14.95
By Sheila Swan & Peter Laufer
"A cache of valuable advice."
—*The Christian Science Monitor*

THE FEARLESS SHOPPER $14.95
How to Get the Best Deals on the Planet
By Kathy Borrus
"Anyone who reads *The Fearless Shopper* will come away a smarter, more responsible shopper and a more curious, culturally attuned traveler."
—Jo Mancuso, *The Shopologist*

SHITTING PRETTY $12.95
How to Stay Clean and Healthy While Traveling
By Dr. Jane Wilson-Howarth
A light-hearted book about a serious subject for millions of travelers— staying healthy on the road—written by international health expert, Dr. Jane Wilson-Howarth.

GUTSY WOMEN (2ND EDITION) $12.95
More Travel Tips and Wisdom for the Road
By Marybeth Bond
Packed with funny, instructive, and inspiring advice for women heading out to see the world.

GUTSY MAMAS $7.95
Travel Tips and Wisdom for Mothers on the Road
By Marybeth Bond
A delightful guide for mothers traveling with their children—or without them!

Destination Titles

ALASKA $18.95
Edited by Bill Sherwonit, Andromeda Romano-Lax, & Ellen Bielawski

AMERICA $19.95
Edited by Fred Setterberg

AMERICAN SOUTHWEST $17.95
Edited by Sean O'Reilly & James O'Reilly

AUSTRALIA $18.95
Edited by Larry Habegger

BRAZIL $18.95
Edited by Annette Haddad & Scott Doggett
Introduction by Alex Shoumatoff

CENTRAL AMERICA $17.95
Edited by Larry Habegger & Natanya Pearlman

CHINA $18.95
Edited by Sean O'Reilly, James O'Reilly & Larry Habegger

CUBA $18.95
Edited by Tom Miller

FRANCE $18.95
Edited by James O'Reilly, Larry Habegger & Sean O'Reilly

GRAND CANYON $17.95
Edited by Sean O'Reilly, James O'Reilly & Larry Habegger

GREECE $18.95
Edited by Larry Habegger, Sean O'Reilly & Brian Alexander

HAWAI'I $17.95
Edited by Rick & Marcie Carroll

HONG KONG $17.95
Edited by James O'Reilly, Larry Habegger & Sean O'Reilly

INDIA $19.95
Edited by James O'Reilly & Larry Habegger

IRELAND $18.95
Edited by James O'Reilly, Larry Habegger & Sean O'Reilly

ITALY $18.95
Edited by Anne Calcagno
Introduction by Jan Morris

JAPAN $17.95
Edited by Donald W. George & Amy G. Carlson

MEXICO $17.95
Edited by James O'Reilly & Larry Habegger

NEPAL $17.95
Edited by Rajendra S. Khadka

PARIS $18.95
Edited by James O'Reilly, Larry Habegger & Sean O'Reilly

PROVENCE $16.95
Edited by James O'Reilly & Tara Austen Weaver

SAN FRANCISCO $18.95
Edited by James O'Reilly, Larry Habegger & Sean O'Reilly

SPAIN $19.95
Edited by Lucy McCauley

THAILAND $18.95
Edited by James O'Reilly & Larry Habegger

TIBET $18.95
Edited by James O'Reilly & Larry Habegger

TURKEY $18.95
Edited by James Villers Jr.

TUSCANY $16.95
Edited by James O'Reilly & Tara Austen Weaver
Introduction by Anne Calcagno

Footsteps Series

THE FIRE NEVER DIES
$14.95

One Man's Raucous Romp Down the Road of Food, Passion, and Adventure

By Richard Sterling

"Sterling's writing is like spitfire, foursquare and jazzy with crackle...."   *—Kirkus Reviews*

ONE YEAR OFF
$14.95

Leaving It All Behind for a Round-the-World Journey with Our Children

By David Elliot Cohen

A once-in-a-lifetime adventure generously shared, from the author/editor of *America 24/7* and *A Day in the Life of Africa*

THE WAY OF THE WANDERER
$14.95

Discover Your True Self Through Travel

By David Yeadon

Experience transformation through travel with this delightful, illustrated collection by award-winning author David Yeadon.

TAKE ME WITH YOU
$24.00

A Round-the-World Journey to Invite a Stranger Home

By Brad Newsham

"Newsham is an ideal guide. His journey, at heart, is into humanity."   *—Pico Iyer, author of The Global Soul*

KITE STRINGS OF THE SOUTHERN CROSS
$14.95

A Woman's Travel Odyssey

By Laurie Gough

Short-listed for the prestigious Thomas Cook Award, this is an exquisite rendering of a young woman's search for meaning.

ForeWord Silver Medal Winner — Travel Book of the Year

★ ★

THE SWORD OF HEAVEN
$24.00

A Five Continent Odyssey to Save the World

By Mikkel Aaland

"Few books capture the soul of the road like The *Sword of Heaven,* a sharp-edged, beautifully rendered memoir that will inspire anyone."

—Phil Cousineau, author of The Art of Pilgrimage

STORM
$24.00

A Motorcycle Journey of Love, Endurance, and Transformation

By Allen Noren

"Beautiful, tumultuous, deeply engaging and very satisfying. Anyone who looks for truth in travel will find it here."

—Ted Simon, author of Jupiter's Travels

ForeWord Gold Medal Winner — Travel Book of the Year

★ ★